T0308869

Frank Lloyd Wright's Forgotten House

Frank Lloyd Wright's Forgotten House

How an Omission Transformed the Architect's Legacy

Nicholas D. Hayes

THE UNIVERSITY OF WISCONSIN PRESS

The University of Wisconsin Press
728 State Street, Suite 443
Madison, Wisconsin 53706
uwpress.wisc.edu

Gray's Inn House, 127 Clerkenwell Road
London ECR 5DB, United Kingdom
eurospanbookstore.com

Printed in the United States of America
This book may be available in a digital edition.

Library of Congress Cataloging-in-Publication Data
Names: Hayes, Nicholas D., author.
Title: Frank Lloyd Wright's forgotten house : how an omission transformed the architect's legacy / Nicholas D. Hayes.
Description: Madison, Wisconsin : The University of Wisconsin Press, [2021] | Includes bibliographical references and index.
Identifiers: LCCN 2020038863 | ISBN 9780299331801 (cloth)
Subjects: LCSH: Wright, Frank Lloyd, 1867–1959. | Elizabeth Murphy House (Shorewood, Wis.) | American System-Built Homes. | Architect-designed houses—Wisconsin—Shorewood.
Classification: LCC NA737.W7 H39 2021 | DDC 720.92—dc23
LC record available at https://lccn.loc.gov/2020038863

For my love,

Angela,

who teaches that art is freedom

Contents

Foreword

Close reading of a house pays off. Since Angela and Nick Hayes bought the Elizabeth Murphy House in Shorewood, Wisconsin, in 2016, they have taken the time to pay attention to the detail of place. This extends from how the sun moves across the living room in the course of a day or year to the quality of the joinery of the house's built-in cabinets. The first type of attention allows them to appreciate the artistry with which the house was designed; the second allows them to piece together clues to the fraught process of its construction—a process that Nick Hayes describes in detail in this book.

The Murphy House is one of a small group of houses designed by Frank Lloyd Wright known as American System-Built Homes. Wright created the System in partnership with Arthur L. Richards, a Milwaukee developer. Wright's goal was to bring fine architecture to as wide an audience as possible. To do that, he developed a system of precut building components that could be marketed on a large scale. Perhaps twenty of the American System-Built Homes are known to have been built, though that number may grow as additional buildings are discovered. Only recently has real study been focused on Wright's American System-Built project, in spite of the nearly one thousand drawings relating to almost 130 American System-Built models in the Frank Lloyd Wright Foundation Archives. After Wright pulled out of the project in 1917, he seems never to have mentioned American System-Built Homes again. Because the records in Richards's office were destroyed after his death, there is little to go on besides Wright's drawings, early promotional material, and hearsay.

While in its early life the Elizabeth Murphy House was known to be a Wright design, by the 1970s that heritage was forgotten, and it was not until 2015 that investigations led to recognition that it is a Model A203 American System-Built Home. Since then another American System-Built Home has been identified in Madison, Wisconsin, suggesting that additional models may surface.

Hayes lays out in detail the dissolution of the American System-Built Homes program and in doing so raises basic questions about the creation of a work of art. Can a system whose goal is large-scale production provide a work of art? While some scholars may debate that question, Hayes's fine description of the spatial qualities of his house can be offered as evidence that Wright's creativity is certainly not absent from the individual American System-Built houses.

Hayes investigates the mystery of the house's disappearance from the Wright canon. As with any good mystery, the story of the Murphy House has its cast of characters, its clues, and its red herrings. While Frank Lloyd Wright is a significant player, the cast also includes Arthur Richards, Wright's partner in the American System-Built Homes project; Elizabeth Murphy, the developer who commissioned the house; Herman Krause, the carpenter with whom Murphy contracted to build the house; Russell Barr Williamson, Wright's young employee who oversaw much of the American System-Built Homes process before going into independent architectural practice in Milwaukee; and last and perhaps most unexpectedly, Alfred and Gladys Kibbie, the home's first occupants, who lived in the house for twenty-four years with their family.

The Kibbies were unhappy with their Wright-designed house. It was too small for their growing family. Family lore indicates that their dissatisfaction extended to the house's designer. Was it Wright's fault that the Kibbies could not afford a larger house? No, but Hayes suggests that Wright came to realize the drawbacks of the System's design process, which lacked a direct architect-client relationship and that he chose to abandon that process as soon as this became clear to him.

Over the next decades, Wright would continue to work on the problem of making fine architecture more affordable. This effort culminated in the development of the Usonian house in the 1930s. With the Usonian system, Wright turns the design process around. Instead of mass-producing building components, he developed standardized details. These details were then used to provide unique designs for each client. The ASBH project, while perhaps being something of a false start, provided Wright with important experience and was a significant step on the path that led to his seminal design for the first Usonian home, the 1936 Herbert and Katherine Jacobs House in Madison. The importance of the Jacobs House in the development of modern domestic architecture has been recognized by its inclusion as one of eight Wright buildings inscribed onto a UNESCO (United Nations Educational, Scientific and Cultural Organization) World Heritage List called "The 20th-Century Architecture of Frank Lloyd Wright."

Hayes's research into the Elizabeth Murphy House contributes to the study and the stewardship of Wright's legacy.

Barbara Gordon is the executive director of the
Frank Lloyd Wright Building Conservancy.

People to Know

Frederic C. Bogk—customer of Frank Lloyd Wright and Arthur L. Richards

Shirley du Fresne McArthur—author of *American System-Built Homes in Milwaukee* (1983)

Juanita Ellias—author of the thesis "Prairie School Architecture in Milwaukee: Russell Barr Williamson" (1974)

Dorothy Hoffmann—best friend of Teddy Kibbie

Richard G. Johnson—Wrightophile and amateur historian looking for lost Wright works

Alfred and Gladys Kibbie—owners of house at 2106 East Newton Avenue from 1918 to 1942

Mary and Virginia (Teddy) Kibbie—daughters of Alfred and Gladys Kibbie

Herman F. Krause Jr.—carpenter-contractor and builder of house at 2106 East Newton Avenue (1917–18)

Mike Lilek—curator at the Burnham Block and American System-Built expert who in 2015 confirmed house at 2106 East Newton Avenue as Wright-designed

Arthur R. Munkwitz—business colleague of Arthur L. Richards and buyer of American System-Built apartments

Elizabeth Murphy—real estate investor who commissioned construction of Wright-designed house at 2106 East Newton Avenue (1916) and for whom the house is named

Lawrence Murphy—husband of Elizabeth Murphy

Arthur L. Richards—real estate developer and partner of Frank Lloyd Wright in the sales and supply of American System-Built Homes

Harold Richards—Arthur Richards's younger brother and partner in the real estate business

Traci Schnell—architectural historian

William Allin Storrer—author of *The Architecture of Frank Lloyd Wright, A Complete Catalog* (1974)

Russell Barr Williamson—employee of Frank Lloyd Wright from 1914 to 1918 and architect from 1914 to 1964

Pat and Roger Wisialowski—owners of the home at 2106 East Newton Avenue from 1993 to 2016

Frank Lloyd Wright—architect and designer of the home at 2106 East Newton Avenue, Shorewood, Wisconsin

PART ONE

How to Find a House by Frank Lloyd Wright

1

The Announcement

So rare is the announcement of a new dwelling by Frank Lloyd Wright that this one made national news in 2015. The headline for an Associated Press story in the *New York Daily News* blared "Wisconsin Couple Discovers Home Was Designed by Frank Lloyd Wright" over a photograph of Roger and Pat Wisialowski looking like lottery winners as they posed in front of their modest cottage.[1]

There was a grand unveiling and a media open house with press releases, photo shoots, and speeches.[2] Wright researchers who had gathered records and evidence to support the announcement were on-site with easels of drawings and historic documents. A tour was offered, and busloads of "Wrightophiles"—experts, academics, conservationists, and fans—arrived to get a peek at the interior, which hadn't been seen by the public, ever.

The house was quirky, covered with modern siding in Cape Cod colors and hidden behind big bushes, but it had signature markings of a Wright design: long overhangs, a front door on the side, walls of windows, and a wide chimney. The dense Wisconsin village of Shorewood is sprinkled with homes in the Prairie style, some rumored to be Wright's but none officially attributed to him.

Intrigued by the headlines and local gossip, neighbors drove past, took selfies, and reported what they found to friends and other neighbors.

It appeared, from the sidewalk, that Pat and Roger were indeed holding a winning lottery ticket. Imagine living in a home for more than twenty years when someone knocks on your door to ask for permission to conduct research and then proves, with substantial physical and documented evidence, that Frank Lloyd Wright was its architect. Pat was quoted as saying that she had sensed the house was special but thought that if there was a Wright connection, it must have been an indirect one. Perhaps one of his students drew it. Another article claimed that the lucky owners would be able to sell the home for "at least 40% more" than market rate.[3]

Pat and Roger immediately listed the home for sale, but their ticket didn't have lucky numbers. Roger soon passed away of the cancer he had been battling for some time. Pat received a couple of tepid offers that unraveled due to issues with financing or questions about condition. The house languished unsold for months despite a hot seller's market. At the time, neighborhood homes for sale were being snatched up at higher than asking prices, but not this one. Lacking interest, Pat paused the selling effort for a few months to take stock and then relisted with a more modest asking price.

A home designed by Wright can be hard to sell. Jokes about leaking roofs raise immediate suspicion, but serious inquirers will consider deeper consequences. Taking ownership of a historic site and building also means taking on stewardship and curation responsibilities for something that many people, especially Wright followers and art and architecture aficionados, consider hallowed ground. Prospective buyers may worry about limits imposed by advocacy groups, governments, or social pressures. Every Wright home is a tourist destination and will be the subject of drive-by photographers. These private places land publicly on Google maps and smartphones and on lists of "things to see while visiting." Local governments and businesses like the inbound traffic, but neighbors worry about congestion and trespassing. Mounting factors narrow the number of possible acquirers.

Furthermore, Pat's Wright-designed home was atypical for its place: small at just 960 square feet, with two ten-by-eleven-foot bedrooms and one tiny bathroom, and located in Shorewood, Wisconsin, where most homes are at least twice the size and have room for a family of four or more. Shorewood is a vibrant urban village, a suburb contiguous to Milwaukee and a destination for aspirational young and growing families who appreciate its walkability, bustling shops, churches, restaurants and taverns, parks and beaches, and especially its stellar public education system. (The Supreme Court Justice William Rehnquist, the tenacious female war photojournalist Dickey Chapelle, the global musical phenom The Violent Femmes, and Hollywood's Zucker brothers are all alumni of the acclaimed education district.) Most folks wanting to buy a home in Shorewood expect more space than Wright had designed and Pat had to offer.

And most important, a *newly* discovered home by Frank Lloyd Wright is itself a puzzle. How does one lose such an important object? We might assume that even in the course of one hundred years, records, images, and memories would remain and that every person connected with it would have taken at least basic steps to secure its pedigree, if not out of economic self-interest as owners, then simply through the colorful lore it would encourage among neighbors.

Instead, sometime between the mid-1970s, when the house was last called a Wright design in a real estate listing, and 1993, when Pat bought it, everyone simply forgot what it was and the house stood nondescript and hidden in plain sight.

In 2016, more than a year after the home was rediscovered, my wife Angela and I felt like lottery winners when we made the home our own. It was a perfect fit for us at the time. Our two daughters were grown, we were downsizing, we were already Shorewoodians, we could offer a fair price considering the pros and cons, we were handy and curious, and we thought we were ready to take on a stewardship effort.

To our surprise, in addition to adopting and moving into a piece of historic art, we also found ourselves drawn into a tangled and muddled mystery by stumbling routinely upon odd inconsistencies and exclusions in the contracts, records, workmanship, stories, and artifacts in and about the home. As we uncovered clues, they began to unfold as a rare untold story; one that sheds bright light on the home's disappearance and, more important, on a lesser understood and dark period in the famous architect's life.

Frank Lloyd Wright is among the most studied persons in modern history, ranking with royalty, generals, presidents, inventors, and stars of the screen in near-cosmic celebrity. This special status comes in part from his vast genius and colorful personality, but it is also a product of his proclivity for self-promotion. Wright liked to talk about himself and his work. Rarely did he distance himself from one of his ideas.

That, however, is exactly what he did with his Model A203, now called the Elizabeth Murphy House, in Shorewood, Wisconsin. It is a rare, uncharacteristic omission, and in its rarity deserving of scrutiny if we are to understand the life of the man, the arc of his career, and the impact and evolution of his ideas and work on our world.

Most studies of Frank Lloyd Wright depend on what he said or wrote about himself and his work. Others cite the memories of his apprentices and clients. This book will tell the story of the work that Wright was determined to censor, the acquiescence of his contemporaries in the cover-up, and what would eventually become of the secret.

Here, we offer new findings as a contribution to the legacy of the world's most famous architect. To do that, we must start by understanding how a house by Frank Lloyd Wright can be lost in the first place.

2

Hidden in Plain Sight

Newton Avenue west of Maryland Avenue in Shorewood is little more than a side street in the center of Wisconsin's densest urban neighborhood. It is too narrow to allow parking on both sides and too unimportant as a thoroughfare to carry much traffic. It also feels unplanned, like most urban neighborhoods of the period. The houses, yards, and trees are eclectic and walks crooked after a hundred Wisconsin winters. The lots are narrow and the buildings tightly spaced. Sometimes neighbors share a driveway. There is a row of sided Milwaukee duplexes in various stages of landlord-disrepair, all built between 1920 and 1940. A pretty brick two-family flat stands out as Moorish and out of place. On the south side there are bungalows, a mid-twentieth-century modern duplex, a fairy-tale stone cottage, and a home that may have once been the farmhouse that predates the development of the area, beginning in the first decade of the twentieth century. That house is now covered in vinyl siding and a bright silver metal roof. The neighborhood is quiet, safe, and unassuming, the kind that might be found anywhere in the aging urban Midwest. It is not one to suggest fine architecture.

If you turn onto the street from Murray Avenue on the west end searching for a Frank Lloyd Wright design, as many do, you may think you are in the wrong place. You drive slowly up a hill, and when you reach the top, something special and different emerges on your right. A tall, wide white chimney adorns a low-slung hip roof supported by four concrete vertical piers rising from ornamented pedestals and separating lead glass windows. Two tall, narrow window slits bookend the row of piers, presumably to add interior ambient light while not requiring shades. Two large square platforms buttress the main wall like altars, supporting great urns for flowers. Between them, a semicircular garden anchors the house to the front yard and the yard to the house. Lacking a front door, the monolithic facade and its narrow window slits are reminiscent of Wright's nearby Bogk House and even Unity Temple in Oak Park, Illinois. The tiny house appears like a jewel among coarse stones.

But it is not the place you are looking for.

In fact, the Eggers Bungalow, built in 1921 in the Prairie style, was designed by Russell Barr Williamson, not Frank Lloyd Wright. Williamson worked for Wright for almost four years before opening his own practice, so the home is in the Wright lineage but it is not a home by Wright.

This was our exact experience as we drove by in the summer of 2015 to see the newly discovered Wright-designed house that was making national news. I recall admiring the white bungalow and declaring, "That must be it!" Angela corrected me and pointed 180 degrees in the opposite direction: "No, dear, that's it."

The Elizabeth Murphy House sits kitty-corner to the Eggers Bungalow across the street, less than a hundred steps away, and is, frankly, much harder to recognize. So, at first blush, it is not surprising that the house by Wright fell off the radar for more than forty years.

First, the house occupies a space that is uncharacteristic of a Wright design: it fronts a narrow, high, deep city lot and is tucked tightly between and in the shadows of two older Milwaukee two-story Victorians with less than ten feet separating the buildings on the east and west.

It is perched atop a hill, in violation of Wright's principle that a proper house placement is "of the hill," not on it.

The awkward, shallow front yard is a steep pitch of grass and shrubs from which the house—a long, flat, windowed box—rises abruptly. From the walk, only twenty feet away but twenty feet below, it feels as though you are looking up at the bridge of a lake freighter and you wonder, but can't see, whether the captain is looking down on you from above.

Despite its diminutive size, the house is imposing and seems to be flexing muscle. Broad-chested with wide shoulders supporting a massive chimney. Doorless. Confusing.

And the house has been camouflaged. When we first came upon it, it was blocked by a tall, dense row of bushes. Whereas other Wright designs of the period feature stucco as the predominant exterior surface, this one was covered in cedar-shake shingles, which had been painted, at least since the 1970s, in a drab inverted color scheme. Wright's usual earthy dark brown stained trim had been overpainted with bright white, framing inorganic blue-gray shingles, so some people had mistaken the house as a Cape Cod.

Finally, the house seems more modern and brutal than it should be, straddling a walk-level driveway anchored by large concrete retaining walls leading to a garage door that is completely out of place.

Because the house originally had no driveway, garage, or carport when it was built in 1917, and because it had no room on either side to add a driveway, a basement garage was excavated in the 1970s, enabling owners to pull a car under the house to park.

Purists view the garage addition as lamentable; a "significant alteration." Cosmetically, they are right. The front facade is different from Wright's vision because the area below grade is now exposed. It's akin to that teenage trick where an eyelid is folded back and sticks. There is also a philosophical problem: Wright is said to have hated garages. He thought they were places to collect clutter.

Once you take the time to see past the changes and study the house, however, key features pop and sparkle. A long built-in flowerbox anchors a bank of eight south-facing windows that reflect the overhead sun, like a chalice holding a flaming light. Horizontal bands carry your gaze from side to side. Because there is no front door, you have to decide which side of the house you will explore first, and you might give both sides equal consideration. The actual front door is completely hidden and is closer to the back of the house, so it is both a mystery to be solved and a hike to find.

These details, in addition to many more in the interior and in the basement (which we will discuss later) were the clues that helped researchers identify and confirm the house as a Wright design in 2015.

Their work, however, was met with some skepticism. When the author of a local Wright fan-club website posted images taken during the first tour, one commenter speculated that Russell Barr Williamson had been cheated of credit for the work he had done designing the house while in Wright's employ. The claim was quickly quashed by a couple of Wright historians, but it did deepen our mystery.

In fact, on the day that we moved into the Elizabeth Murphy House, we began to wonder about the Williamson house across the street. Something didn't make sense. A quick Internet search for the name Russell Barr Williamson turns up impressive titles including "partner to," "protégé of," "associate of," and "supervisor of architectural planning for" Frank Lloyd Wright. It would seem harder, not easier, to lose a house designed by Frank Lloyd Wright standing near a structure designed by someone with close affiliation to him, as this one does. We found ourselves asking, again, how a house by Wright—and specifically one a stone's throw from another historic and well-documented property—could be lost in the first place. With daily inspiration from the Eggers Bungalow seen from our front window, we decided to learn more about the people who were working on and around East Newton Avenue during the time of the design and construction, and, if we could, create a timeline of their involvement.

Perhaps the exercise would help answer our question.

Timelining necessitated reading as much as we could about Wright in and before the period of the American System-Built project so that we could know the man who had designed our tiny forgotten home.

3

Wright's America

While visiting rural Italy in 1909 and 1910, Frank Lloyd Wright admired the simple stone Gothic and classical structures. However, he called Renaissance spaces in modern cities unnatural and demoralizing. Greek and Roman columns used after the ancient Greeks and Romans were not neoclassical, they were bad copies. This was doubly true in America—a still new world that Wright hoped to shape—a place with infinite potential for creativity and innovation but so far hampered by nasty habits of impatience, banality, and plagiarism.

He wrote, "The democracy of the man in the American street is no more than the gospel of mediocrity."[1] In other words, the American experience, in Wright's view, was culturally shallow and unenlightened, which manifested in shallow and unenlightened built environments.

So he made it his mission to stop the "unfair use of borrowed forms" and the "endless string of hacked carcasses" popping up in New York and other American cities trying to be like New York and Rome and Paris before.[2]

This was a lifelong challenge that Wright accepted from his mentor Louis Sullivan, who had found his own architectural training at the Massachusetts Institute of Technology (MIT) in 1872 "to be merely academic" and "quite according to rule."[3] Sullivan left MIT after only one year because he had learned that most American architecture solved no problem but instead imitated the classics, as if imitation itself were sacrosanct. Sullivan rejected this idea outright and thus posthumously earned the title the Prophet of Modern Architecture, in large part because Wright took and carried his baton. Sullivan taught Wright that art in architecture was rooted in creative solutions resulting in fresh experience and that there is no art in a copy.

Wright was determined to find inspiration in places other than ancient Athens and Rome, casting a wider net to assemble more suitable elements into something he called "absolute individuality" and "organic integrity."[4] Through commissions for opulent custom homes such as Robie House, Hollyhock House, and Fallingwater; via large public spaces such as Midway Gardens and the Marin County Civic Center; in places of worship such as Unity Temple, Annunciation Greek Orthodox Church, and the Unitarian Meeting House; and for buildings of business such as the SC Johnson Research Tower and Great Room, Wright found patrons—one after another—willing to support and pay for his better vision and version of America.

Wright believed that the vast American lands and vistas should inspire the design of the cities, villages, and homesteads that would be placed on them. About his own expansive Taliesin in Spring Green, Wisconsin, Wright wrote, "There must be a natural house, not natural as caves and log-cabins were natural, but native in spirit and making, with all that architecture had meant to make whenever it was alive in times past."[5] Organic design was from the earth up and in parallel with it, an expression of natural beauty and individual freedom and his interpretation of the American dream.

In a 1957 interview with Mike Wallace on national television, Wright, then ninety, famously declared that given enough time, he could redesign all of America and that America still desperately needed to be redesigned. He acknowledged a lifelong, persistent frustration with everyday American people and their drab everyday choices. In that interview he said, "I think the common man is responsible for the drift toward conformity now. It's going to ruin our democracy."[6]

The Wallace interview was more a reflection of experience than an expression of a late-life plan. During his nearly eighty-year career Wright made two concerted attempts to create something fresh and different for folks without the means to afford original art: the American

System-Built Homes, designed in the Prairie style and built between 1915 and 1917, and his famed Usonian homes, designed from 1936 until his death in 1959. The American System-Built Homes effort was short-lived, and its history remains spotty. His Usonian designs, however, played a large role in assuring his legacy. Some Usonian homes were built even after his death. Some of Wright's Usonian clients loved the homes enough to dedicate their lives to finding ways to protect them for posterity.[7]

The American System-Built program, of which the Elizabeth Murphy House is the last completed home, was an experiment in mixing art with manufacturing—or at least the methods of manufacturing that enforced standards to ensure speed and quality. By engineering rules into such common items as windows, doors, foundations, and joists, Wright was searching for and experimenting with efficiencies that could bring economies of scale in both cost and time to the construction of a home, potentially opening a market for modest but lovely spaces into which those confounding common men and women might fit.

Wright thought that standardization might speed the work of house building to an American pace and lower the cost to a widespread affordable price. But the art—his architectural contribution, creative solutions, and the fresh experience of organic design—would make American life better.

In a speech to potential investors and builders in Chicago in 1916 that was meant to launch the American System-Built program, Wright said:

> I have had faith in the machine as a characteristic tool of my times, and therefore an artist's tool. I believe that this tool put into an artist's hand could be a real benefit to our civilization.[8]

Here we find repeating themes in Wright's lifelong philosophy and work. All of America, not just its wealthy, needs *his* version of purposeful and lasting design, but American economic, social, and political systems (and, indeed, most of its citizens) are too impatient and distracted by life's pace and daily demands to appreciate and embrace it.

Experimentation—with new tools, ways, and methods like machines and markets—might be a means to artistic democratization.

His first attempt to deal with this problem was to look for efficiencies in the supply chain without sacrificing his craft. It was a business model solution to a market problem akin to the big-box retail store, which buys in bulk, controls the product and price, and delivers everywhere.

Wright could not do this alone from his studios in Chicago and Taliesin. He would need a factory and a sales and distribution system. He partnered with the Milwaukee real estate businessman Arthur L. Richards, a man with a track record of development in the new subdivisions springing up in growing midwestern cities.

It is telling that Wright's first foray into the delivery of homes for the common man and woman claimed "American" and "System" in its brand. After all, America was both an artistic opportunity and a mess needing to be cleaned up; and at the time, Americans were solving problems with systems such as manufacturing with interchangeable parts and pieces.

As we will see, Wright would learn that American ingenuity and systems were often as messy as its people.

4

The Americans

In 1918, Alfred and Gladys Kibbie were newlyweds and looking to settle where they could start and raise a family. Alfred was employed as a valet at the Trostel Tannery on Water Street in what is now called the Upper East Side of Milwaukee. Three miles north, Shorewood was becoming a destination neighborhood; a perfect prototype of the new American subdivision. It had been called East Milwaukee until 1917, when it was rebranded to invoke images of the tree-topped bluffs overlooking gold sand and stony beaches along Lake Michigan to the east. On the west, the Milwaukee River ran parallel to the lakeshore, north to south, and train tracks ran parallel to the river. There had been a water park with its own trolley stop—a midwestern version of Coney Island—featuring beer gardens, a rollercoaster, and a waterslide that launched its sliders into the cool, gentle river. Though the amusement park was closed in 1916 as the water dirtied with accelerating development and a growing population, trolleys still carried city dwellers north to the area for the river and lakeside parks.

A fine public school system was built. There were police and fire departments, bustling shops, modern roads and sidewalks, places of worship, electricity and city sewers, and a popular lakefront country club.

As houses popped up near the trolley stop, city dwellers snatched them up to become suburbanites, commuting south to jobs downtown. Streetcars crisscrossed the neighborhoods from east to west, connecting the villagers.

In December 1918, the Kibbies responded to a classified ad in the *Milwaukee Journal* that read:

> UNIQUE SHOREWOOD BUNGALOW, NEW AND READY FOR OCCUPANCY. Located at 440 Newton. Originally designed by Frank Lloyd Wright. Has open floorplan, living room, breakfast nook, kitchen. 2 bedrooms, _ wardrobes and 2 coat closets. Large porch, electric light fixtures, hot water heat, stationary wash tubs, hardwood floors, stucco exterior, lot 50×135, price $_500. Terms extremely easy. Open for inspection Sunday from 2:__ to 5:__. Other days by appointment or Phone Edgewood 2721W.[1]

The Kibbies were excited about the location, the price, and the easy terms. They were not excited about the architect.

In 1918, Frank Lloyd Wright was mired in his lowest period, a decade of tumult and tragedy. He had built but then bankrupted his Chicago practice. He had left his first wife, Catherine, and six young children to travel with Mamah Borthwick, his mistress and the wife of a former client. Negative publicity haunted him. Regular clients abandoned him. He lived a triple life for years: one life in Chicago keeping his kids fed and propping up a failing practice; another in his new home and studio in Spring Green, Wisconsin, on which he had borrowed to build; and a third on the road, as he frequently traveled abroad for the sparse work coming his way.

His beloved Mamah was murdered at Taliesin in 1914, along with her children and some of Wright's staff, and Taliesin was destroyed by the murderer-arsonist. Wright would borrow again and again to rebuild Taliesin, while his business continued to suffer. His celebrity as an innovator had dulled. His reputation as a narcissist and philanderer was acute. His main focus was on the design of the Imperial Hotel in Tokyo, but in order to complete it he would routinely leave the country for Japan to serve a Japanese emperor. Much of the project work would fall to him because few of his staff would follow for fear of not being paid.

That he had designed a home in Shorewood that the Kibbies could afford to buy was inconsequential.

But, consequentially, Elizabeth Murphy, the real estate speculator who had commissioned and was selling the house, had extended credit to the newlyweds. The Kibbies purchased the house from Murphy on a land contract rather than a mortgage, which meant making payments to Murphy rather than to a bank. It was a common financing scheme at the time, and it was the only way the young couple could pull it off.

Indeed, the Kibbies did start and raise a family in the home. They had two daughters, Mary and Virginia, or "Teddy" for short. The family lived in the home from 1918 until they sold it in 1942, the year after Teddy graduated from Shorewood High School.

Stories passed down by the girls and their friends helped us understand the family's relationship to the famous architect.

Dorothy Hoffmann (née Stock) was a member of the Shorewood High School class of 1942—a junior when Teddy was a senior. She and Teddy were members of the Girls Reserves Club, among other social organizations at school and in the neighborhood, and were and remained best friends throughout their lives.[2] They did almost everything together. However, Teddy had not once invited Dorothy into her home. We were introduced to Dorothy by Kathy Kean, a volunteer at the Shorewood Historical Society. When Dorothy visited us in the summer of 2016, she was ninety-one years old, and it was the first time she had set foot in her friend Teddy's house, although she had lived nearby her entire life and played in the yard countless times as a kid.

Dorothy described the Kibbies as quiet, proud, kind people without a lot of money. Mary and Teddy were beautiful, smart, and popular. Mary was a member of the "S" Club, an organization promoting sports for girls. Teddy was in the orchestra. Both Kibbie girls worked on the *Shorewood Ripples*, a prestigious school newspaper, studied foreign languages, and earned high grades.[3] Their parents, Gladys and Alfred, were welcoming and generous and would take the girls and their friends on weekend trips to swim in and picnic near the warm, clean inland lakes southwest of Milwaukee. Gladys became president of the Atwater Parent Teacher Association, leading campaigns to invest and reinvest in Shorewood's fine public schools; was a member of the Shorewood

Women's Club; and was active in the Shorewood Welfare Association, which, among other things, put on plays, readings, and concerts to raise funds to "aid the needy."[4] They were happy people, Dorothy said. "But there was not any happiness in that house."[5]

Dorothy remembered that Teddy "hated the house," a view that she had inherited from her mother. The neighbors all lived in houses with distinct rooms and front doors. Passersby could see clear through the Kibbies' window-clad house, but it was not clear whether there was a door at all. Most Wisconsin homes had tall gables and steep-pitched roofs to shed snow. The Kibbies' low-slung house looked as if it belonged in Tokyo, not Shorewood.

The family adapted. Dorothy recalled that Teddy once told her that she shared a tiny (ten-by-eleven-foot) bedroom with her sister, Mary, and their frail grandmother, who suffered from dementia. Teddy and her mother planned Teddy's high school graduation party to be held at a friend's house instead of their own.

Their hatred ran deeper than inconvenience. Much later in their lives, Dorothy and Teddy and their husbands took a driving trip to the East Coast, passing through Pennsylvania on the way back. Wright's famed Fallingwater was open for tours when they were in the area. Dorothy suggested that they stop and see it. The husbands agreed. Teddy sat in the car stewing, refusing to give Frank Lloyd Wright and his most celebrated work a minute of her time.

Dorothy told us that Teddy called Frank Lloyd Wright an "immoral man."[6]

A picture from 1929 suggests that the Kibbies had taken deliberate steps to hide their Frank Lloyd Wright–designed house. The open-to-the-air sleeping porch had been closed with sashed windows and heated. The passage to the front door via the sleeping porch had been closed with a locking door. The main windows were covered with blinds and shades. The cedar-shake shingles on the roof had been removed and replaced with diamond-shaped asbestos shingles. In addition to covering the roof pitches, those shingles were extended up and around the huge chimney, which had originally been sheathed in stucco. Finally, the front facade was partially hidden by shrubs and no

Alfred and Gladys Kibbie's Frank Lloyd Wright–designed American System-Built Home Model A203 in 1929. Photo courtesy of Shorewood Historical Society, donated by Dorothy Hoffmann.

flowers occupied the flowerbox, though that may have been because of the time of year when the photograph was taken.

Another picture from the mid-1930s indicates a quicker pace to cover up the remaining Wrightian features. In only a few years, all the exterior stucco had been overlaid with siding, the windows were overhung with large bulky awnings, and the entire front of the house was blocked by large shrubs.

The Kibbies had removed the cantilevered wings that spread from the flowerbox crown, a signature Wrightian decoration of the time. They may not have liked the look, or perhaps the wings blocked the shrubbery. Incidentally, in 2018, we re-created these cantilevers. We selected the proper wood and took exact measurements from photos and renderings. We thought that internal bracing—grids visible only from the top down—might have been designed for structure or for hanging baskets.

Appraisal photograph from the late 1930s. Courtesy of Shorewood Village Assessor.

However, with some time to study the effects, we have learned that Wright's main objective was to cast moving shadows on the front of the house; a light and shade metaphor representing the draping plants that would hang from the box in the summer and that emphasizes light, nature, and the horizontal. The whole house is lifted up on a sunny day by these contrasting shadow grids.

Why remove signature Wrightian elements? Were the Kibbies embarrassed?

One Sunday afternoon while working wood putty into a century of nail holes in the trim banding the living room, we found a clue, hidden in plain sight. All the exterior windows of the house had been outfitted with common pull shades—the familiar fabric rolls that would yellow and warp in time. (These shades are clearly visible in the photo from 1929.) They would have been pulled down either to block the sun or for privacy at night. Although we've since removed all window treatments,

Elizabeth Murphy House front facade in 2019. Photo by Nicholas Hayes.

some of the hardware and scars from nails that once held hardware remain. Between the living room and what was designed as a sleeping porch and front entryway, there is a bank of five glorious art glass casement windows; a ten-foot-wide by seven-foot-high wall of light shimmering through leadwork and blown glass. When the sleeping porch was an open unheated porch, the windows provided a gentle sight line to the outside from all corners of the main house, a classic Wrightian feature. When the sleeping porch was enclosed and heated, the window bank was demoted to a decorative glass partition separating two parts of the usable interior space. The layering, light, sight lines, and art glass designs remain, but the function is less important.

Remnant hardware and nail holes reveal that shades had been installed on what had become a glass wall. Why block the view between a living room and a sunroom or den? No outsider sees in through these panes, and they are not a source of harsh direct sunlight.

We don't have the exact date that the porch was enclosed, but we know that it was sometime before 1929, either when or soon after the house was being completed or during the first ten years of the Kibbies' time here, when three generations were squeezing into the space.

The fact that the Kibbies once pulled shades to block the view through these windows suggests that the enclosed porch had been repurposed not as a den or a sunroom but as a bedroom—probably a large *master* bedroom for Gladys and Alfred.

This house was small for a family of five, and they needed more room than they could afford. By turning a porch and entryway into a bedroom, however, they also created an awkward social situation: anyone entering the house by the main door would have to walk through the home's most private space.

Frank Lloyd Wright designed experiences for the people who entered his spaces. He hid the door to force visitors to find it. And by creating a deliberately small space through which one must pass before reaching a larger space, he caused a temporary quieting followed by the feeling of freedom that comes with the pleasant surprise of relative spaciousness. The method is famously called *compression and release*.

The Elizabeth Murphy House boasts two waves of compression and release. The first comes at the porch entryway leading into the sleeping porch, and the second comes after passing through the original main door and through a narrow passageway into the living room and the heart of the house in front of the hearth.

A Kibbie guest would have to find the entry, be compressed while passing through it, and then release (surprise!) into Gladys and Alfred's bedroom, undoubtedly resplendent with Gladys's knickers or Alfred's boxers.

It is no wonder that Dorothy had not been invited to come in. No one other than family could be allowed.

The Kibbies' solution was practical, messy and clumsy, and annoyingly limiting: not what Wright had planned and not what a friendly, modest American family of five living in a close-knit and up-and-coming neighborhood would have in mind for their ideal home.

5

The Tour

You can see the entire Elizabeth Murphy House in three minutes. It is tiny.

But there are places to pause and experiences not to miss.

Once you find the entry, you will notice that two people cannot enter the front porch at the same time. The passage is too narrow and steep. It asks you to step in single file, be quiet, deliberate, and think about what is coming next. A friend of Japanese descent entered for the first time, head intuitively bowed, and then looked up, smiling and surprised, and declared: "I've just passed through a Torii gate . . . leaving the mundane to enter the sacred."[1]

At that moment, you will be struck by the dramatic views opening on three sides. On your right, a window vista frames the garden with a giant draping balsam tree shading a bed of ferns and a long grassy yard. If it is a windy day, branches will dance for you at eye level. A squirrel may scurry below. On your left, time recedes and a curious history begins to unfold. The unpainted walls and ceiling are covered in shiny pebbles that twinkle bright white and rainbow hues. The space is too large and strange to take in all at once. The ceiling is especially intoxicating: a seamless carpet of tiny jewels stretching thirty feet. We often doze on a soft rug on the porch floor to study the faux twinkling stars above and invite guests to try too.

However, you've not yet entered the home. Though you can see into it from the porch through that bank of once-shaded floor-to-ceiling

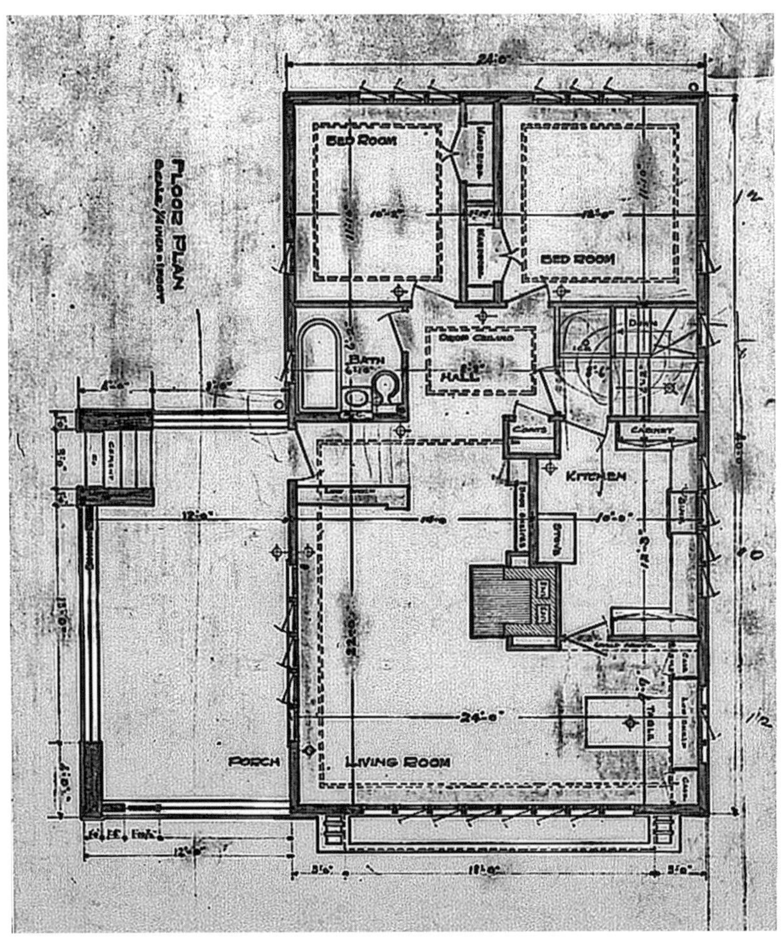

Path of entry and location of the Place of Greeting in the Model A203 (drawing reversed from built version). American System-Built (Ready-Cut) houses for The Richards Company, Floor Plan, Frank Lloyd Wright Foundation Archives, 1506.301.

Sleeping porch interior with art glass, front door, light, and pebble-dash exterior surface. Photo by Sara Stathas.

windows, you can't make out the plan. If a fire is lit in the fireplace on the other side of the windows, you will be drawn to it, so you search for and find another passage, then pass one by one through another narrow walkway into the living quarters.

As you pause to shed your hat and coat and be welcomed—something that usually happens in a foyer—you are now standing in the very center of the house and formally beginning your relationship to the space and its people. This is a point worth repeating: most greetings in most dwellings happen at the outside edge of the social space. In the Elizabeth Murphy House, you are greeted as guests while you are standing at the heart of the home. You have completed your journey and are inside with friends; warm, safe, attentive, and welcome. We have come to call this spot the Place of Greeting for its powerful social impact and symbolism.

At the Place of Greeting and with your hellos complete, you are compelled to decide: Are you feeling sociable? If so, you will be drawn left,

Katherine Hayes, daughter of the author, in the living room with its hearth and south-facing windows. The roof of the Eggers Bungalow is visible through the windows. Photo by Sara Stathas.

where the spaces are sunlit and soar up and out and you will find more friends and lively conversation. Or are you feeling quiet and introspective? If so, you will be drawn right, where the space is more circumscribed and intimate.

You are persuaded by a dramatic change in the scale of the spaces that you are seeing and the contrasting acoustics that you are noticing. It is a bit like standing at the edge of a cliff and choosing to either dive into the cool water below or walk backward and leave the splash for another day. The living room on your left is expansive, tall and inviting. The voices and music are clear. The fire crackles. The hall ceiling on your right is deliberately low, almost cramped, and still, magnetic. If you are six foot six or taller, you will need to duck to enter. In the hall, sounds are hushed and the light dims, and you face a maze of six doors that open into the two tiny bedrooms and the bathroom, a coat closet, the passage to the back door, and a linen cabinet. The hall is not a place for conversation. In fact, when you reach one of the rooms meant for sleep or personal care, your senses have been calmed simply by making a three-step journey through the hall.

Visiting architects from Spain told us that they call this the choice between day and night. We have noticed that, left unprompted, introverts will turn right and extroverts will turn left. The left turn experience is also worth having.

When you enter the high-ceilinged living space, you will first feel obliged to pause and stand near the fireplace mantel to take in the views. You will discover a long row of south-facing windows and a breakfast nook bookended by handsome tall cabinets with glass doors featuring an organic art glass motif—perhaps roses or a tree—at eye level. The cabinet doors are mirrored by the same motif in the floor-to-ceiling art glass windows that draw your gaze back to the porch from which you came, and the same moniker—the logo for and theme of the

The five-foot partial wall shielding the entryway creates compression before release. The varying ceiling elevations—ten feet in the living room, six and a half feet in the hall—ask the person standing at the Place of Greeting to choose between social and intimate spaces. Photo by Sara Stathas.

Breakfast nook built-in cabinet. Photo by Sara Stathas.

space—bookends the eight tall windows on the southern wall. Here again you will connect with nature. This is the spot in the home from which you can see out in all directions. North, a dense Wisconsin woods and prairie. East and west, homes with nearby neighbors and friends. South, an expansive city skyline that connects the home to the walk and the street and that connects you to the community.

Your hosts will then invite you to take a winding path into the kitchen for some refreshment; perhaps a glass of wine or some cheese. Unlike kitchens in most American homes, you won't linger in this one. While functional, bright, and smart, it is too small for more than one person to work at one time. You will be soon ushered out, and like a magnet, you will be drawn back to the fireplace to start another conversation.

There, you may run your fingers along the bricks and feel that they can travel only left or right. The specifications called for the face brick "to be laid as indicated by detailed drawings in a workmanlike manner with white mortar, and horizontal joints being raked out ⅜″ back from face of brick and shall be laid to a ⅜″ joint with the least possible vertical joint."[2] Wright insisted that the grout in the vertical seams of the fireplace masonry be smoothed to the brick surface, while grout in the horizontal seams be inset, creating an effect of horizontal stripes, as opposed to stacked cubes. It was another way to draw your focus left and right, to the people around you. Incidentally, it is a brickwork technique that Wright used throughout his life. Inset horizontal grout joints can be seen on the outside walls of later Usonian houses, pulling whole homes lengthwise.

Nearly everything you have experienced during your tour was intentional. Wright planned every step, every view, and every feeling. In fact, you might also sense that he is now influencing your conversation. You will be talking about history, or places you have visited, a concert you have seen, or friends you have recently met, but you won't be talking about *things* because there are few things to talk about. Wright didn't make room for anything but a few rows of books and a couple of paintings.

It is widely known that Frank Lloyd Wright scorned Greek Revival and Victorian designs with their dark cluttered rooms and halls crammed

Art glass details in the row of windows between the living room and sleeping porch. Photo by Sara Stathas.

with thick drapery, cabinets, tables, lamps, and stuffed couches. Indeed, sparsity is the essence and the ethos of the American System-Built Home, and especially this tiny Model A203. Wright didn't want the place to be filled with junk.

Coincidentally, we landed here because of a burning desire to downsize. We had hoped to shrink our footprints for some time. Wright made it an imperative.

The house in which our daughters were raised was a 2,300-square-foot brick Dutch Colonial just eight blocks north on a friendly street near the grade school. Like most Shorewoodians, we had moved to the village for the schools, picked the biggest house we could afford in 1994, and then stuffed it full of the things that American families collect: toys, books, furniture, tools, bikes, linens, appliances, dishware, instruments, stereo gear, TVs, computers, iPads, heirlooms, antiques . . .

You get the point.

The Elizabeth Murphy House is 1,200 square feet *if* you include the sleeping porch as living space, but the main house is just 960 square feet. The two bedrooms are each just large enough for a double bed and a chest of drawers but nothing else. There is no cabinet or shelf in the bathroom for a towel or extra bars of soap. The basement is functional, with a utility room and a place for hanging laundry, but storage space is at a premium.

There are four small closets, just enough room in dining and kitchen cabinets, and one small bookshelf. To make space for ourselves in the home, we sold, gave away, or threw away half of our possessions. That work is ongoing. Moreover, the work to reset our lives to fit Wright's scale and plan is ongoing too.

We've observed two new material behaviors as we adapt to new proportions.

First, we have become highly selective about what we keep and display. Never-to-be-read books don't make the shelf-space cut but go to a library or a used book store. A picture must mean something to get a nail. Sometimes a decision to install a thing—like a towel hook, for example—takes weeks. Often the decision is no. A hook may have utility, but if it breaks the flow of a line, form overrules function.

Second, we have found a new rhythm in a refreshing and restorative routine that a friend coined "just-in-time living." Instead of stocking up on staples or getting more of something that we might need because we happen to be at the store (fasteners, toothpaste, mulch, or milk), we have learned to consider our immediate need and buy only what is required. The result: we spend less, store less, maintain less, waste less, and consume less. Burdens are shed. And we have more time.

It should be said that "just-in-time living" could be a choice—something anyone can do. Frank Lloyd Wright helped us see it, but we don't see living any other way from this day forward. We recommend it to everyone.

It is here that the Japanese influence on Wright's designs is most obvious and most clever. In his 1943 autobiography, Wright reflected that he had found American habits and Japanese philosophies to be contradictory:

> The direct application of their ancient Shinto religion would see most of our [American] domestic arrangements tumbled out of the windows into the street, a rich harvest for some junk man.

Despite that contradiction, Wright was determined to experiment on everyone who would step foot in this space—to shrink our American lives in order to expand them. His study is ongoing, 102 years later, though it could not be more timely:

> Spiritual significance is alive and singing in everything concerning the Japanese house. A veritable song. And it is in perfect unison with their heaven.[3]

Before our first tour of the Elizabeth Murphy House, our idea of downsizing was but a trendy notion, the next adventure for a couple of lucky baby boomers. We knew the trappings and triviality of living an American consumption lifestyle and wanted out. What we could not know, until entering Wright's brilliantly judicious and manipulative space, is that small is indeed beautiful, sparsity is divine, and friends should always be greeted from, by, and at the very center of the heart.

6

The System

> American System-Built Homes have not been given their rightful place in architectural history. They have been accused of "not being supervised by Wright," "being a flop," "having extremely marginal construction" and being in "impossible" locations.

So begins the conclusion of Shirley du Fresne McArthur in her 1983 book titled *Frank Lloyd Wright: American System-Built Homes in Milwaukee*. While significant additional research and attention have been given to the American System-Built program since her book, it remains the most in-depth collection of records and analysis of the program and deserves credit for shining a bright light on the historical significance of Wright and Richards's brief collaboration. She counters naysayers by adding that "the outbreak of World War I right at the time American System-Built Homes were introduced, and Wright's long stay in Japan, followed by the public's fancy for the bungalow, halted development on a concept Wright continued to support during his lifetime."[1]

That there would be a need to defend any of Wright's creations as historic or consequential seems purely pedantic, but there are understandable arguments on both sides about the program's right place within his body of work, given his sparse subsequent references to it. But much was said and written about it as the idea was being developed.

In the 1916 Chicago speech touting American System-Built Homes, Wright claimed the System as his own. He expected it to deliver nothing less than quality design and workmanship.

> The idea of the American System has been in my head for years. I have guarded it carefully. I wanted time to think in quiet of how the idea might be brought to the public without injury to the integrity of my own art.

He also claimed it would be novel:

> I believe the world will find in the American System of house construction the only instance in the world today of a work which has absolute individuality due to a central idea which is the organic integrity of the work.

And he said that his System would be transformative:

> Somehow in America, architecture has never been appreciated. We are perhaps the greatest nation of house builders in the world, and the most slipshod nation of home builders. . . . Now, I believe that this coming of the machine has so altered the conditions of home building that something like this American System was inevitable, but I have not borne in mind purely the economic side of it. . . . Simply selling houses at less cost means nothing to me. To sell beautiful houses at less cost means everything.[2]

Wright's claims were confirmed by his partner in the program, Arthur Richards. In a promotional brochure, Richards credited Wright with both beautiful designs of homes and the invention of the scheme of logistics and premade parts to make them well and fast. He said, "[Wright] has really done what no other modern artist has even dared to do. He has achieved the touch the old craftsman had—the beauty that cannot die, by the use of modern building material mills, modern labor, and modern commercialism, the machine."[3]

The American System-Built program is rarely mentioned by Wright biographers, but when it is, it is unquestionably Wright's innovation—his concept and his ideas about mass shelter on display—albeit for a short, transitionary, and mysterious time. In his 1942 book *In the Nature of Materials*, in a chapter about the years 1911–20, Henry-Russell Hitchcock said, "[Wright's] technical genius expended untold pains on the details of such a tremendous low-cost housing scheme as the Ready-Cut houses and apartments."[4]

Wright's idea needed to be marketed. Under the terms of their agreement, Richards would be "engaged in the buying, selling, manufacturing and erecting of so-called Standardized System Built buildings in all parts of the United States, Canada and Europe." To do this, The Richards Company would procure, prepare, and deliver everything needed to build a house, furnishing "the plans, drawings, specifications and details and lumber, mill work, exterior plaster material, paints, stains, glazing, hardware trimmings and electric lighting fixtures."[5]

Wright was to be employed and retained "for the purpose of drafting, designing, making and completing all of the designs, plans, specifications and details . . . to be by [the Richards Company] sold and manufactured."[6] Richards would be licensed to enlist subcontractors: dealers to sell and carpenters to build the houses. In this way, he would be able to reach cities all over the United States with the program, riding a building wave that was subdividing farmland contiguous to fast-growing urban areas and turning those lands into neighborhoods. Advertisements show Richards aligned with fourteen dealerships and at least seven carpentry contractors near a Chicago branch office, and the list would grow.[7] Because his main office was already in Milwaukee, he would be the local agent in that city.

Richards would be contractually disallowed to alter any of the plans or designs, though Wright's plans included choices—options and upgrades that Richards could offer to prospective buyers, such as the style of the roof, cabinet layouts, or the addition of a separate carriage house. Richards would have the right to call Wright to prospective areas—towns and neighborhoods and tracts of land—to assess suitability for development, though it is not clear whether this ever happened.

The partners expected the products to be in high demand and the partnership to be lucrative. The contract required that Wright would be paid a total of $7,500 in three $2,500 tranches over the first six months to cover the costs to create and release a vast library of drawings and instructions. Wright would also receive at least $250 per week to start and up to $500 per week plus 3.5 percent on the first million dollars in sales and 1 percent on additional millions over the first million dollars.[8]

However, sales didn't happen quickly enough, so royalties and commission payments never materialized as anticipated.

Much later, critics would remark that without direct supervision to interpret the ideas, inspect the quality of materials and workmanship, or to select plots and place homes organically on them, Wright was leaving much to chance.

When forced to work remotely, an architect's arbiter of advice and the main means to control quality are the comprehensive drawings and specifications and detailed materials lists and instructions that they deliver to the builder. In fact, Wright and his team produced more than nine hundred drawings for the program, seventeen of them for the Elizabeth Murphy House alone. Some experts have said that the American System-Built project was the largest single design effort Wright would undertake in his life. As we will see, the effort, while huge, was insufficient.

Moreover, despite his large investment in plans, processes, and man-hours, Wright was quick to cancel the entire thing when he began to understand the true scope and nature of the work, the price of volume production, the risks in a multilayer distribution network, and the barely trickling flow of cash when sales started slowly.

Du Fresne McArthur points out that Wright "didn't credit the buildings publicly" after his contract with Richards had been canceled. In fact, Wright skipped over the program in his own autobiography, moving from the completion of the Midway Gardens in Chicago in 1914 to the design and construction of the Imperial Hotel from 1915 to 1923 with short sidebars to reflect on the rebuilding of Taliesin after the fire, his second marriage, and his interest in Japanese prints.[9]

In his book *Frank Lloyd Wright: The Lost Years, 1910–1922*, the architect, educator, and historian Anthony Alofsin gives only a paragraph to the program, despite there being more than one hundred model designs created by Wright during the period (more than 10 percent of his lifetime output).[10] Because Wright didn't write about the American System-Built Homes, it has been difficult for anyone to footnote or reference their historical significance by quoting him.

That does not mean Wright had not learned much from the experience. Lessons from the program seem to inform the second half of Wright's career and his most fantastic creative works. We will explore these connections and consequences in more detail later. For now, let's look at one small piece of evidence that Wright did not completely forget the good elements in his canceled System and instead retained them for future use.

An image found in the Avery collection at Columbia University, the newly designated warehouse for the largest collection of Wright drawings and letters, includes a page signed by Wright, dated September 1918, a year after the program had been canceled. On it, Wright wrote, "Revision of 'American System' to produce characteristic *wooden* ~~type~~ style of building. *Grammar—'Wood.'*" He was moving forward while gathering up a few of the better ideas to store for later.

Artists don't omit the art that did not sell from their memories or their collections. They simply don't market those pieces and instead reuse the good elements and set aside the bad.

In her book about the American System-Built Homes in Milwaukee, du Fresne McArthur reflected, "Frank Lloyd Wright did not lose his interest in the idea of contributing to low cost housing for the average American family."[11] Indeed, Wright wrote a two-page letter to the *Architectural Forum* in 1938, saying that "I would rather solve the small house problem than build anything else I can think of."[12]

He may have missed an opportunity to find small house solutions at 2106 East Newton Avenue.

Wright never set foot in the Elizabeth Murphy House, and he never met the Kibbies. It is not a stretch to imagine that Wright and Gladys Kibbie would not have gotten along. Yet by not having had the

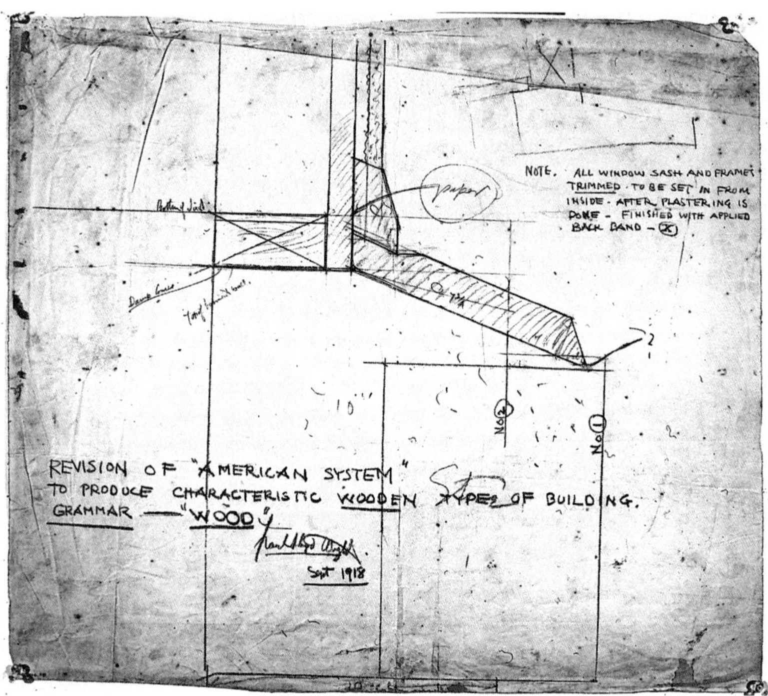

Frank Lloyd Wright's 1918 post-project reference to "American System" on a sketch bearing his signature. American System-Built (Ready-Cut) houses for The Richards Company, Notes in Red Crayon, Frank Lloyd Wright Foundation Archives, 1506.058.

experience of seeing the yard and the house and meeting its occupants, Wright missed a key opportunity to learn what he might have done differently to make a home that would meet the needs of a couple of modest means who were planning a family. As we have seen, in the case of the Kibbies, easy terms made purchase possible; mismatched design was the problem from then on.

As you might now expect, Wright never mentioned the home, and the Elizabeth Murphy House isn't mentioned in du Fresne McArthur's book either. Nor are the people who were involved in building, selling, buying, or living in the home.

Wright's omission may have been wholly intentional, as we will soon see. Du Fresne McArthur's omission was likely unintentional. Her book was written during the period that the house was in hiding. However, by not knowing about and therefore not being able to pursue clues and evidence that would be found only at 2106 East Newton Avenue, du Fresne McArthur couldn't know or compile the complete American System-Built Home story.

7

The Timeline

Let's walk through related events leading up to and including the construction of the Elizabeth Murphy House. (The chronology at the back of the book also includes key events from this chapter.)

Arthur L. Richards and Frank Lloyd Wright were not strangers when they agreed to build American System-Built Homes. Richards had commissioned Wright to design a hotel (that was not built) in Madison, Wisconsin; they worked together on a hotel project in Lake Geneva in 1911; and they had other deals in the works in and around Milwaukee.[1] Initially, they flirted with a "System" when Richards speculatively built a model neighborhood featuring three of Wright's designs on a block on the Near South Side of Milwaukee starting in October 1915—now called the Burnham Block for short. Richards had purchased a tract of land that normally would have been subdivided into four front lots but instead packed ten family units onto the block by cutting it into six smaller parcels and then building and eventually selling four identical duplexes and two small single-family homes. These six structures are the main subject of Shirley du Fresne McArthur's book and are in various stages of decay, preservation, and protection.[2]

Richards was also in partnership with one Arthur R. Munkwitz. The entrepreneurial Munkwitz family were amassing a variety of businesses and properties in and around Milwaukee. Arthur R. Munkwitz, son of the German immigrant butcher Charles Munkwitz, was the president of the American Realty Service Company, where Arthur

Richards was vice president. Their working relationship would have been close by any measure.

In September 1916, Munkwitz and Richards hired a carpenter contractor named Charles Koth to build a block of apartments—American System-Built Model J-521—on Twenty-seventh Street near Highland Avenue on Milwaukee's Near West Side that the Munkwitzes would put up for rent. Russell Williamson was the site supervisor on the project. The buildings were demolished in the 1970s to widen the road.

Richards was not only involved in building structures that he and his colleagues might rent or sell, such as the Burnham Block and the Munkwitz Apartments. When Richards met a neighbor of Munkwitz who was looking to build a new home, Richards persuaded the man to purchase architectural services from Frank Lloyd Wright and he then brokered the deal.

Frederic C. Bogk had done well in railroading and forest land sales in northern Wisconsin and was a Milwaukee alderman. The home he commissioned from Wright through Richards would make a statement. It would sit proudly atop the Lake Michigan bluff among a row of luxurious lakeside homes overlooking the beach and exuding fine living. It would be three thousand square feet and feature interior details designed by George Mann Niedecken, himself a master artisan of glass and furniture and a trusted collaborator of Wright. The house was to cost $15,000, which, it should be noted, was a bargain. The equivalent in 2020 dollars is just under $400,000. Today the Bogk House is priceless and historic and stands out among houses without Wrightian DNA to the north and south that are valued in the millions.

Much later, in 1955, Wright would call the Bogk House "a good house of a good period for a good client."[3]

Williamson would play a major role in its construction, and, as history now shows, the experience imprinted deeply on him.

In her 1974 master's thesis, the art historian Juanita Ellias observed that drafting styles seen in the Bogk drawings suggest that Williamson may have drawn some of the Bogk home while working in Wright's Chicago studio. She noted that, "at one point in the development of the design, the Bogk House's exterior bore the simplicity of Williamson's style," with one version "provided [presumably by Williamson] with a flat roof, simple coping, and bold, plain corners."[4] In fact, the house would be built with a hip roof, not a flat roof, to make room for an attic in which to hang laundry, and other drawings reveal the edit. She wondered, however, how much of the project should be fairly attributed to Williamson.

Shirley du Fresne McArthur picked up the theme to show that later plans by Williamson for a "square house" are themselves a close copy of plans by Wright for a "fireproof" house.[5] Ellias also notes "striking similarities in the details found in the Bogk House and many Williamson Houses."[6]

We see those similarities every morning in the Eggers Bungalow across the street.

Here we confront an uncomfortable architectural reality: the fact that one artist influences another even though a design idea may rightly belong to one and not the other. Where does originality end and copying begin? How do artists in the employ of other artists express their own work? How do artists who employ others to execute their ideas retain ownership?

Our timeline was teaching us about lineage. Who is related to whom? Whose ideas are related to whose?

We were also learning that original art isn't scalable. It can't be manufactured. It can be replicated, but then it isn't original art anymore. It is a copy. A single artist may create from experience and call that work original, but artists who team with others can't easily make the same claim. And when an artist leaves another in charge of the work, ideas spill onto the floor for anyone to pick up.

Moreover, there *was* another artist in charge of the work in our neighborhood during some of the time that our home was being built. Russell Barr Williamson, like du Fresne McArthur, Wright, and the Kibbies, would also omit the Elizabeth Murphy House from his personal narrative. In a memoir written by Williamson's son and granddaughter after his death, there is no mention of work done at 2106 East Newton Avenue, despite sixteen Williamson-designed homes within a half mile built between 1919 and 1924, within six years of the Kibbies moving in. Three Williamson homes are within *250 feet* of the Elizabeth Murphy House, including the Bogk-like Eggers Bungalow directly across the street.[7]

It was becoming clear to us why this house by Frank Lloyd Wright was lost. Nobody wanted to talk about it. It had been orphaned as a toddler by everyone associated with it while second- and third-generation cousins appeared, one after another, after another.

PART TWO

How to Lose a House by Frank Lloyd Wright

8

The Afterthought

We first set foot in the Elizabeth Murphy House as potential buyers. We scheduled a time to tour with the listing real estate agent and had the experience that Frank Lloyd Wright planned for us one hundred years earlier.

First, we searched for and found the door. Then, we compressed and released twice. Once in the home, we immediately felt its soft energy, admiring the layers, lines, and finishes that are remarkably well preserved given its age.

We recall sensing a singular spirit in and of the space. Although small, it feels much larger. Although open, it is also private and intimate. Without electric lights turned on, every nook is bright enough with just daylight. Although organized, it is unpredictable. Every corner reveals another pleasant surprise. Every station anchors a glorious view. We knew we wanted to live in the home two minutes into our three-minute tour. Condition had quickly become unimportant. It was easy to see through synthetic treatments like linoleum and plush carpet. Obviously, this place cared for its people but also needed care that we were willing to provide.

The tiny home had self-selected its occupants after the Kibbies. Most came without kids for lack of room for them. For the previous seventy-five years or so, it had been lived in by retirees, single adults, and empty nesters who would not need room to grow. A small, contented adult population acted as a security blanket for the home. The floor plan is therefore unchanged.

Because it would not contain large pets or small children, it would not see extreme wear and tear, therefore many surfaces are original. When you touch the trim, your oils add to years of oil layered on the hundred-year-old shellac. When you knock a pebble from the pebble dash wall, you are erasing century-old work, so you try hard not to do it.

Because its systems were and are basic and modest, the house has been easy and affordable to maintain. The roof, paint, furnace, and water heater have remained functional and modern. The records of care and maintenance are mostly intact.

The bathroom, however, was a boiling, roiling disaster in which another mystery lurked.

Wright's reputation as a designer of bathrooms is not his strong suit. Some observers have said that the water closet was his afterthought. That was the case here. Like the rest of the house, the bathroom is of course small; just 6 by 6½ feet. This, in and of itself, would not be a large problem if not for the placement of the door, per his instruction, to open into the knees of someone sitting on the commode.

To make matters worse, by placing the hinges to the center and the knob on a far corner of the room, the open door sliced the room in half, making it feel like a six-by-three-foot space, with a tub occupying the only remaining walkway. Imagine Mary and Teddy fighting for one small mirror and then being knocked into the tub like dominos by Dad inadvertently opening the door.

Moreover, the bathroom was a nightmare of bad repairs covering bad repairs.

Four layers of linoleum hid decades of toilet bowl floods, and the floorboards had begun to squish. Floods were so frequent that a sub-roof had been added in the basement to divert dripping toilet water away from someone working at the laundry washtub below. A built-in bathtub/shower was placed next to a wooden window, spraying the frame with each use and setting up dry rot. The original plaster had been covered with tile in a variety of materials. Three walls of tacky pink and baby blue plastic tiles merged into a wall covered in white

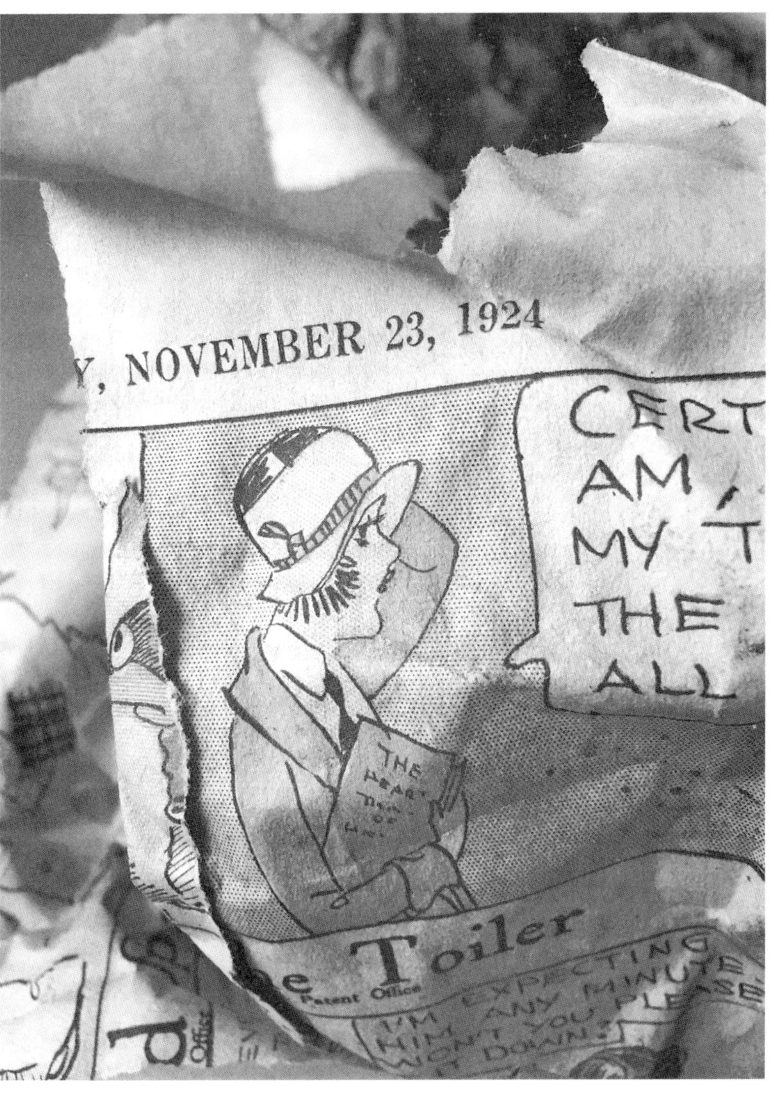

Newspaper fragment from November 23, 1924, found in exterior wall February 27, 2017, during bathroom demolition. Photo by Nicholas Hayes.

ceramic tiles. To hide the mismatched materials, someone brushed light brown latex paint on all the tiles, but the paint ran, dried in globs, and then began to peel. The toilet and sink had been replaced with oversized fixtures from a home center, and a particle board cabinet—one grade less than IKEA—had been bolted to the wall just where your head wanted to be when sitting on the commode, so you had to lean forward not to hit it, which made a potential door-opening event all the more dangerous. In addition to hitting your knees, depending on your proportions, the door might also hit the top of your hunched head and you would rebound to hit the back of your head on the corner of the cabinet, like a pinball between flippers.

We knew that the house would be unlivable until something was done about the bathroom. We developed a plan and gutted the room within weeks of moving in. We took everything out: the fixtures, tile, linoleum, sills, and floor, and began anew from the joists. While vacuuming out dark wall spaces that had been exposed with the removal of the built-in tub, we discovered a curious and confounding artifact.

Whoever installed the tub tried to insulate the wall behind it and had used newspapers to do it. Two *Milwaukee Journal* color comic sections from September 24 and November 23, 1924, were not to be salvaged—they disintegrated with any movement—but also raised an interesting question. Why would there be papers from 1924 in a wall in a bathroom in a house that had been finished just a few years earlier? What conceivably could have gone wrong?

There are two possibilities for this artifact: either the original plumbing had failed fast or the Kibbies bought and lived in a house without a proper tub—or, for that matter, any decent place to bathe—for the first six years.

Fast-forward to today and the new period-appropriate, per-the-plan bathroom is lovely and flows (only figuratively) with the rest of the home. It features an exact model clawfoot tub, proper plaster walls, small fixtures, and, since we reversed the hinges, a door that opens gracefully without cutting the room in half and, thankfully, without knocking into the knees and forehead of a commode sitter.

9

The Delay

On September 17, 1919, more than two years after ground was broken on the Elizabeth Murphy House, a lawsuit was filed in the Milwaukee County Courthouse by Lawrence Conlan, the attorney for the carpenter-contractor, Herman F. Krause Jr., alleging that Krause had not been paid and was due $778. The suit explains that Krause and Murphy had entered into an agreement by which Krause would "erect One American Model A. 203, being a one-story cottage . . . according to Plans, Specifications and Drawings made by Frank Lloyd Wright, for the sum of Thirty-four Hundred ($3,400) Dollars, of which amount Eighty (80%) percent was to be paid from time to time as the work progressed and the balance on completion of said building."[1]

It is important to note that because Alfred and Gladys Kibbie had taken ownership and were living in the house while making payments to Murphy, they were also named in the Krause lawsuit as codefendants. It may have been a legal necessity on the part of Krause's lawyers to also sue the Kibbies, but we can imagine the Kibbies' dismay when they learned that they had been drawn into the conflict. They may not have known, until being served by the sheriff at their front door, that there was a conflict at all.

Two months later, on November 12, 1919, Elizabeth Murphy's lawyer filed an "answer" to the lawsuit on behalf of Elizabeth and her husband, Lawrence, and Alfred and Gladys Kibbie. It alleges a wide range of failures on the part of Krause. Among other things, it claimed that:

- the plaintiff had left the building "unfinished to a considerable extent"
- he "did not furnish . . . screens, a proper plate glass mirror for medicine case, benches for breakfast nook, a scoop shovel or pipe covering"
- "nail holes and cracks [were] not puttied . . . wax finish not given to the interior woodwork . . . and [floors] not oiled and stained"
- "water, during rains, was leaking through the roof at several places . . . and at several windows and caused damage"
- "the rear window and rear entrance door were left in a badly damaged condition"
- "he did not furnish a proper door to the basement entrance."[2]

When Krause walked off the job site on or about October 15, 1918, never to return, he had not yet completed the plumbing, the electrical work, or the heating. The kitchen was incomplete, and there were no finishes on the floors, cabinets, and wood trim.

Murphy's answer also consults language found in the boilerplate contract for American System-Built Homes that she must have read (and presumably signed) at the start of the project. She expected that "in case of any differences . . . the decision of Frank Lloyd Wright, architect, should be final and binding."[3] Krause had not submitted any questions to Wright.

How could he?

Just two months into construction, which had begun on April 20, 1917, Wright terminated his agreement with Richards via letters and his own lawsuit, which preceded the Krause lawsuit by more than a year. From Wright's perspective, the program had ended in the summer of 1917 because he was no longer being paid. During most of the many months that Elizabeth Murphy's house was under construction, Wright considered that he had no responsibility to it—or any other laggard Richards project, for that matter.[4]

Contractors trying to complete their work would have had to fend for themselves.

The lawsuit was not Elizabeth Murphy's only problem. Starting in October 1918, she was faced with the decision to finish construction or sell an unfinished house. Her lawyer claimed that Krause's delays caused Murphy to be "deprived of the use of said building . . . of rental value for approximately eighteen months."[5] Because the Murphys lived in a house just 1,100 feet away and downhill, they probably watched and worried from their back porch as the work started, paused, restarted, and stopped outright and their unfinished investment property stood unoccupied. There would be no profit from their investment.

By November 1918, and with Murphy and Krause still haggling about details, Wright was heading back to Japan to supervise the initial construction of the Imperial Hotel he had designed, and Russell Barr Williamson—once his Milwaukee project supervisor—was no longer with the company, although it should be noted that he had been in the neighborhood in the last months of work under Wright and during the first few months of construction of the Murphy House. We will look at that brief overlap later.

The Krause versus Murphy/Kibbie lawsuit contains dates that supplemented our timeline substantially (see the chronology at the back of the book). Though Wright had sued Richards to cancel the program in August 1917, Krause continued work for sixteen more months, finally quitting in October 1918 as winter was coming on and, in another cruel twist, deaths from the "Spanish flu" pandemic were peaking and many Milwaukeeans were compelled to stay home (a situation that survivors of the twenty-first-century COVID-19 pandemic understand all too well).[6] Murphy was not able to sell her house until August 1919, still in an unfinished state.

We can see that the Elizabeth Murphy House began as an outright fiasco. It was delayed, it was over budget, a blame game was raging, there was no structure—business, people, or processes—to support the project, and it was too much for one carpenter-contractor to tackle. Krause was left holding the bag. He would not receive his $778, losing his 1919 lawsuit against the Murphys and the Kibbies.

Ironically, three contemporaneous nearby Wright-Richards collaborations—the six American System-Built Homes on the Burnham Block, the Munkwitz Apartments at Twenty-seventh Street and Highland Avenue, and the famous Bogk House, with its spectacular Niedecken interior—all took far less time to build than the tiny Elizabeth Murphy House.

How much less time?

Considering the 1924 newspapers found in our bathroom wall, the delays in the completion of the Elizabeth Murphy House may have been long in the extreme. The artifacts suggest two possibilities.

One scenario: the original plumbing was hastily and poorly installed by someone other than Krause in an effort to make the home ready for sale after Krause was gone. That plumbing failed, requiring a major bathroom renovation long before expected. Costs and consequences of the repair would fall to the Kibbies. During deconstruction, we looked for evidence of improperly placed pipework that would support this theory. For example, a hard freeze might have burst pipes run in an exterior wall. The absence of scars to support this theory does not rule it out but weakens it.

An alternate and more likely scenario is that the Kibbies had knowingly taken ownership of an unfinished home and lived in it while slowly finishing it themselves, project by project and as they could afford, for as long as six years or more. Alfred Kibbie may have read the newspaper on November 23, 1924, before crumpling up the comics section and shoving it in the wall to insulate the new bathtub he was adding to the unfinished six-by-six-foot bathroom that he was sharing with his wife, mother-in-law, and newborn daughter.

However it happened, for a young couple without a lot of money but with a packed house into which no guests could be welcomed and with no place to bathe, the Kibbies were living with daily reminders that they had purchased a lemon. This left a sour taste that would last generations.

Moreover, based on the legal evidence, we can see that, like Krause, the Kibbies had fallen victim to the failure of The System. Imagine scratching together enough money to buy your starter home, living without basic working appliances, investing in the fittings and fixtures and sweat equity to make it your own, and then facing cops and lawyers with lawsuits and liens.

We asked Dorothy Hoffmann if she thought the Kibbies had faced legal trouble. "They were too proud and would never bring something like that up," she replied.[7]

Their silence would become a convenient cover for anyone else needing to preserve reputation.

10

The Finding

One of the first people to suspect that the house at 2106 East Newton Avenue was designed by Frank Lloyd Wright, and to act on his instinct, was a hobbyist Wrightophile named Richard G. Johnson, a production manager at the Medill School of Journalism at Northwestern University in Evanston, Illinois. Johnson had been sniffing around Chicago and Milwaukee chasing leads on "lost" homes for years. He was following clues laid out by Dr. William Allin Storrer, author of *The Architecture of Frank Lloyd Wright, A Complete Catalog*, who had published a controversial supplemental list of suspicious homes deemed "The Mysterious 29": extant dwellings that seem Wrightian in their architecture but lack the documentation to confirm their pedigree.[1]

Johnson was also in loose coordination with local historian Traci Schnell, who was part of a group collecting and considering evidence about "Shorewood Houses" as early as 2008. Johnson was the first to knock on the door of Pat and Roger Wisialowski, the occupants of the Elizabeth Murphy House at that time, to share his hypothesis in 2012.[2]

But Johnson was not only trying to find lost homes, he was also assembling clues to support his theory that Wright's activities in the dark time between 1910 and 1920 were not always aboveboard.

Michael Horne writes about architecture and real estate for an online magazine called *Urban Milwaukee*. By happenstance, Horne met Johnson at a social gathering in 2013, and they agreed to tour the area together to look at some of Johnson's finds. Horne described Johnson as a jaunty fellow: red-faced, with billowing white hair, and driving a convertible MG needing a push to start every other time.[3] Horne shared with me part of the email that he sent to his editor: "Richard Johnson, who was at a party here once . . . is coming up from Chicago to give me some architectural news that he seems to think is quite important. Probably of a historic nature, but apparently with a Milwaukee connection."[4]

Johnson picked up Horne one summer morning in 2013, the top down on the MG, and they looked at two dozen homes and buildings in and around Milwaukee, many designed by Russell Barr Williamson. Johnson would leave the home at 2106 East Newton Avenue to the very last; the final dramatic stop—his coup de grâce!—the home that he was convinced was a Wright design and that had been hiding in plain sight.

Horne reflected that there seemed to be a "schism" between Richard Johnson and others studying Frank Lloyd Wright. Johnson suspected that Wright was operating undercover during the dark period, perhaps because Wright's sullied reputation was making it hard to meet payroll. One of Johnson's theories was that Wright was doing the work and asking others to sign it. Alternatively, he wondered whether Wright might have been taking money under the table to shield the origin of the work coming from his struggling studio. Johnson used the word *pariah* to describe Wright—or at least to describe Wright's behavior in those years.[5] These explosive assertions pitted Johnson against a culture of adoration that had formed around Wright and his work in the second half of his career and in the half century since his death.

Horne told his editors that a Milwaukee history group had "dismissed [Johnson] as a kook," even as Johnson was tipping off "the Wright folks who did the conclusive research" that would result in the formal unveiling of the Elizabeth Murphy House. In 2015, when the Elizabeth Murphy House was revealed to be Wright's, Horne tried to reconnect with Johnson but learned that Johnson had passed away sometime soon after their adventure in the MG and would never see the results of his tip-off nor confirm his own controversial theories. Horne wrote about his experience with Johnson in *Urban Milwaukee* and reflected in conversation with me that the article was meant to offer "posthumous vindication" for Johnson.[6]

With the benefit of physical and documented evidence, we now know that Johnson was correct about this house, but it is not clear that he was correct about Wright's behavior, at least in the context of the American System-Built program. The volume of work done to start up the program and the correspondence detailing unpaid bills as cause for terminating it tell us that Wright expected aboveboard payments from his partner Richards and he simply wasn't getting them. And Wright was explicit about his ownership of the American System.

Johnson seems not to have seen all the American System-Built Home archives at the Avery Library, nor had he studied the correspondence, lawsuits, and contracts that explain roles, rights, and payments. If he had, they might have helped him settle his suspicions and bridge the schism between him and other Wright sleuths, which in turn might have provided him with due credit for his find at 2106 East Newton Avenue.

Instead, that credit would go to Mike Lilek, another accomplished Wrightophile who picked up where Johnson, Schnell, and others left off and searched and found the documentation that proved Johnson's hypothesis. Lilek had earned eminence as an expert on the American System-Built program by helping to raise funds to purchase and restore an American System-Built Home Model B-1 on the Burnham Block in Milwaukee, while leading tours as a docent and eventually becoming the curator of the not-for-profit group that is working to buy up and conserve the prototype American System-Built neighborhood for posterity.

Lilek's attention turned to 2106 East Newton Avenue when his mother, Pat Lilek, heard her friend Pat Wisialowski's story during a card game. Pat Wisialowski told Pat Lilek that Richard Johnson had visited and had interesting theories about her home. Pat Lilek recounted the story to Mike Lilek, who was, like most people, skeptical of Johnson and his claims. Given his background, however, Lilek knew exactly where to go to confirm or deny the find. When he arrived to inspect 2106 East Newton Avenue, he went straight to the basement.

Wright's System was about enabling fine architecture within constraints such as space, time, or money. Characteristically, he was thinking about the problem when creating solutions. Because the main challenge of modest home design was to deliver a lovely home at a low cost, many of the methods he created were focused on efficiencies in either materials required or hours needed to assemble those materials, but also, significantly, in the context of light, beauty, and shape.

To do this, Wright developed an innovative and nontraditional foundational modular scheme built on balloon framing spaced twenty-four inches apart instead of the more common sixteen-inch spacing between joists and studs that most American home designers and builders used at the time and still use today. By widening these spaces and strengthening walls and roofs using other means, windows could be placed between studs without headers. This alone would save almost 20 percent in framing lumber and dramatically shorten the time to construct walls with windows. Within his System, a wide range of window heights would be available and would be shipped from the factory complete, including sixty-four, forty-four, thirty-eight, thirty-six, thirty-two, and twenty-six inches tall. By selecting one of these heights in a row or a location, Wright could strategically place his so-called light screens without creating a difficult structural challenge and save time for the builder. As a result, windows could be freely and liberally applied to American System-Built designs: often in long rows to create those screens but also in nontraditional formats, placements, and flows.

With this platform, Wright was able to affordably position seven or eight tall, twenty-four-inch-wide windows in a row, opening spacious views of yards, trees, and birds—an organic luxury. In the Elizabeth Murphy House, there is a bank of eight windows, a bank of five, a bank of four, and three banks of three windows, in addition to two eight-foot-wide openings and one fourteen-foot-wide opening in the porch. The south-facing wall is more window than wall, with twenty-four feet of openings in thirty-six feet of distance. In many models, Wright would place three, four, or five windows in a corner, creating a view from the inside wrapping 270 degrees around the person standing or sitting there. This feature is often found in bedrooms. For the privileged occupant, walking into a windowed corner feels like walking into nature. From a second floor (some models had more than one story),

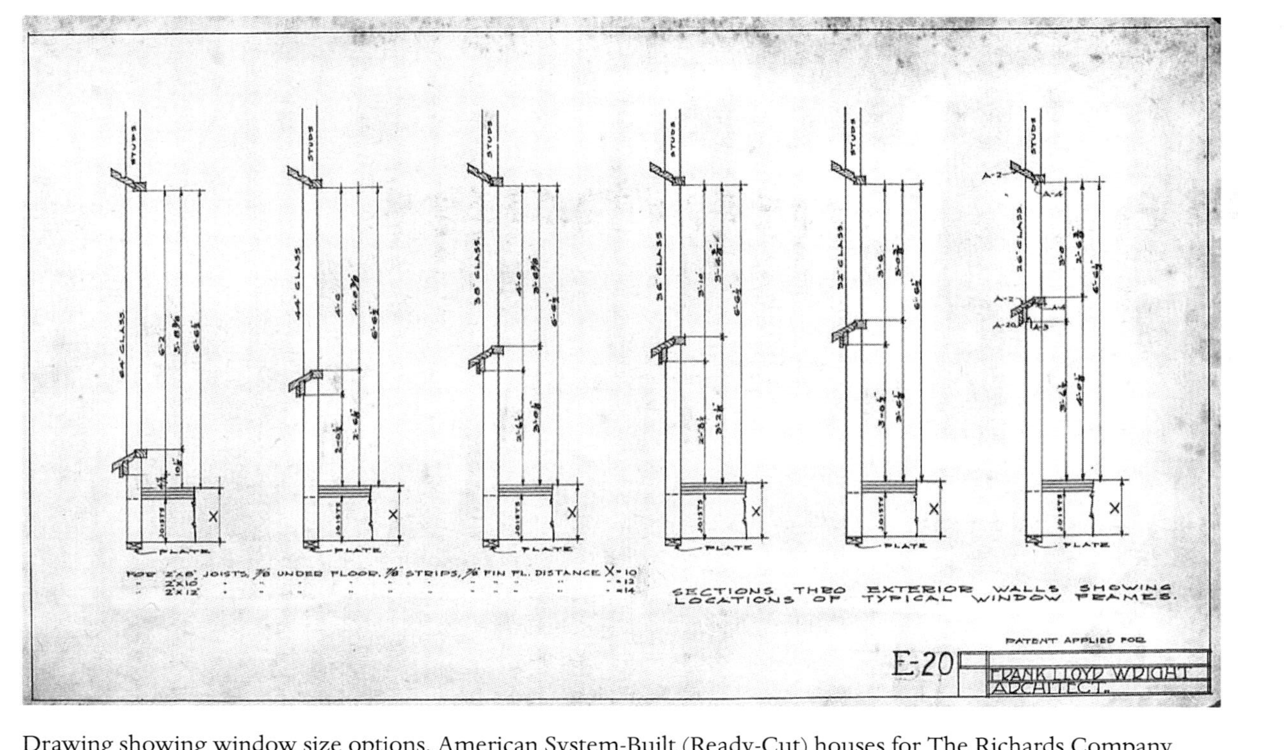

Drawing showing window size options. American System-Built (Ready-Cut) houses for The Richards Company, Millwork Full Scale, Frank Lloyd Wright Foundation Archives, 1506.660.

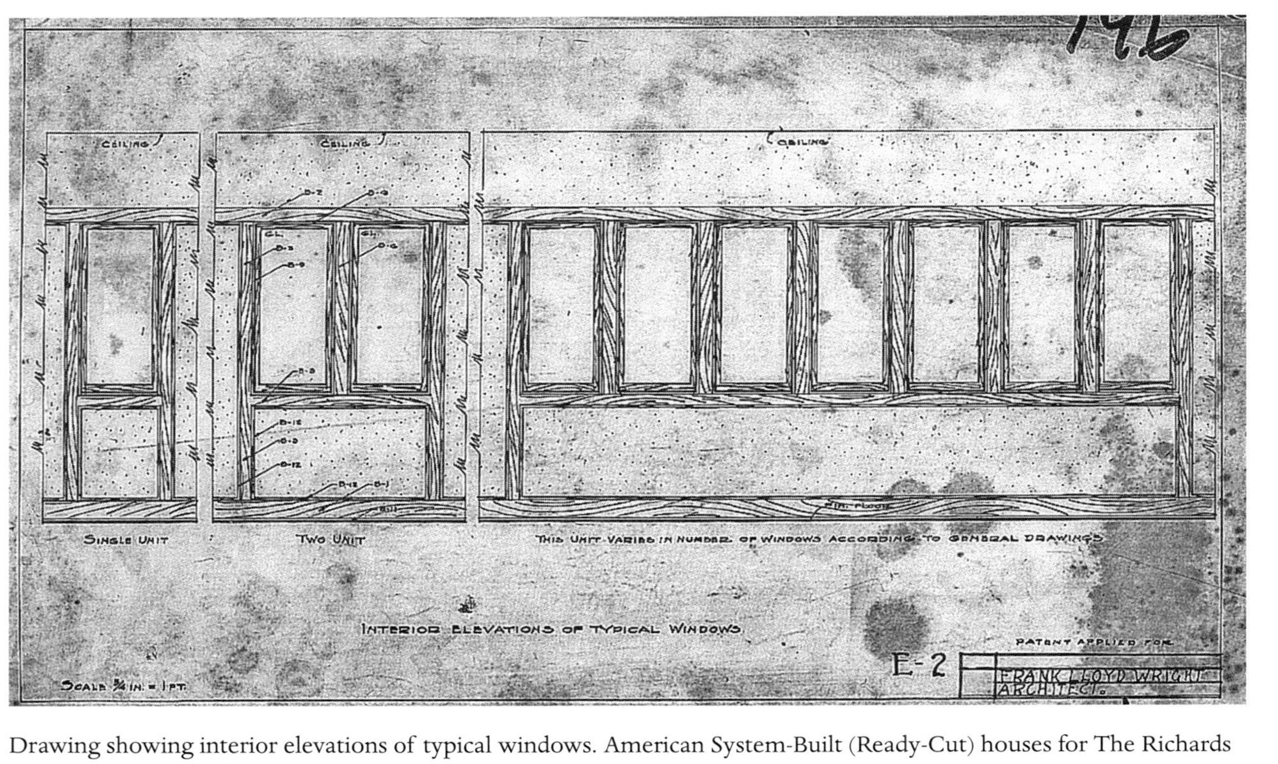

Drawing showing interior elevations of typical windows. American System-Built (Ready-Cut) houses for The Richards Company, Typical Windows, Frank Lloyd Wright Foundation Archives, 1506.748.

one would have a commanding view of the canopy and garden below. On a first floor, it would feel as if you had stepped into the garden without leaving the bedroom. Open corner windows on adjacent walls would create a cooling cross breeze on a warm summer night.

Even today, such features would be seen as modern and extravagant. In 1917, Wright's light screens were space-age before the space age.

Wright's System was both efficient and elegant, enabling the machine *and* the art. It took cost out of materials and time while ensuring original organic beauty in the space. As with the toy blocks designed by educator Friedrich Fröbel—formative during Wright's own childhood—Wright had created patterns, designed templates, and worked out the foundational math to allow new ideas to spring from common shapes and geometries. About Fröbel's blocks, Wright reflected,

> [I was] equipped . . . with the Froebel-kindergarten education I had received as a child from my mother. Early training which happened to be perfectly suited to the T-square and triangle technique now to become a characteristic, natural to the machine-age. . . . The smooth cardboard triangles and maple-wood blocks were most important. All are in my fingers to this day.[7]

Windows were blocks in Wright's American System.

To support his twenty-four-inch walls and windows, Wright specified nonstandard flooring too: two-by-*twelve*-inch floor joists spaced twenty-four inches apart on their centers, as opposed to smaller two-by-ten-inch joists spaced sixteen inches apart that support most floors in most homes. This platform was uniquely specified and built into Wright's American System-Built Homes and was made possible by the last remaining stands of old-growth pine trees in the Wisconsin Northwoods being harvested at the time—an unsustainable resource, running out just as the program was being launched. When Mike Lilek found oversized, overspaced joists in Pat's basement, he knew that Richard Johnson's theory—at least Johnson's theory about who designed 2106 East Newton Avenue—would be confirmed.

A Frank Lloyd Wright–designed home had been found.

11

The Scare

Mike Lilek visited our home again in 2017—a few months after we had moved in—to look at our progress. We talked about our bathroom renovation plans, which were just under way. He predicted we would find hard maple floors under the linoleum, which we did (though they were too far gone to salvage), and he shared the measurements of a clawfoot tub that had been found in one of the Burnham Block properties when a basement was cleaned out. During our subsequent bathroom reconstruction, we would find an exact match on Craigslist to restore, and the tub and bathroom in the Elizabeth Murphy House are finally, after one hundred years, built to Wright's specification (except, of course, for the location of the door hinges, as explained in chapter 8).

We lingered with our guest in the curious sunroom (that may have once been Alfred and Gladys Kibbie's bedroom) to look at the pebble dash walls. Lilek told us that Wright first saw and appreciated pebble dash (also called roughcast) on a visit to San Diego with his son. Lilek said that Wright thought it might work well for the exterior surfaces of American System-Built Homes. The method was popular in maritime climes and praised for low cost, good looks, and uniform durability. Pebble dash starts with plaster applied to brick or lath and, while wet, multicolored pebbles are *dashed* onto the surface and sometimes pressed in with a wet towel. Colors would be whatever you happened to get from the quarry at the time. We see gray quartzite, tan and white granite, and sparkly black biotite.[1]

We compared notes: Lilek reported that the exteriors of the houses on the Burnham Block were all overlaid with siding or shingles within about fifteen years of construction. We shared photographic evidence that this house had shingles over the pebble dash by at least 1933 (also fifteen years after the Kibbies moved in), presumably due to rapid deterioration of the material. Pebble dash over wood lath crumbles during freezing winters because wood and rock don't dance well together. The original exterior treatment remains in our sunroom, however, because almost immediately, someone—either Elizabeth Murphy or the Kibbies—added windows and heat that would protect the walls against rapid expansion and contraction.

As our visit was coming to a close, Mike placed his hand on the pebble dash wall and said in a soft breath, "Have this tested for asbestos."

It was a punch to the gut. We had relied on reports from home inspectors and real estate agents when finalizing our offer to purchase the home, and none of them had called out asbestos in the walls. But Mike was the expert and had worked on the renovation of at least two other American System-Built Homes, so his suggestion was one to be taken seriously. We had noticed that dust was a problem in the tightly windowed room. Every so often a pebble would dislodge from the ceiling and bounce on the floor. We were collecting them. So we wondered: Were we breathing asbestos fibers falling from the layer of plaster under the pebbles when one dropped? We immediately sealed the room from the rest of the house and purchased a small particle air filter to pull dust out of the air while we considered our options.

In addition to saving stud lumber with his innovative balloon construction method, Wright's System would also save money and time and make up structural strength in the methods and materials used to create the interior and exterior walls. Because there would be fewer studs and headers, some of the strength would have to come from the walls themselves. This was atypical for the time (and still is). Whereas most interior plaster walls and exterior stucco walls were built by layering plaster on lath, often nailed to studs by a mason, Wright explicitly called for no lath and instead required the use of a proprietary sheathing that promised to be simpler while providing some weight bearing. The specification says:

> Lathing: No Lathing is to be done by this contractor as building will be sheathed outside and inside with Byrkitt Patent Sheathing Lath. This is to be done by the carpenter.[2]

Patented and marketed starting in 1890, Byrkit was pitched as a stronger, longer-lasting, easier-to-install substrate on which to apply plaster.[3] It seemed an ingenious engineering idea: tongue-and-groove boards were milled with trapezoidal slots into which wet plaster was then pressed, locking the system together, setting and sealing it as it dried. The result was a laminated, interlocked, waterproof wall with incredible strength that was relatively lightweight, as long as it expanded and contracted uniformly. As a bonus, it was hard to ignite, so the home could also be marketed as fireproof. Given Wright's experience with catastrophic fire, this would seem to be an important promise for him to make to clients.

A modern metaphor for the Byrkit concept is the use of closed-cell foam core materials covered in carbon fibers impregnated with epoxy in boats, cars, and rockets. The hollowness creates lightness. Interlocking fibers built up layer upon layer create strength. The uniform thin-walled surfaces create stiffness and structural integrity. The natural metaphor is the egg, which is thin-walled and hollow too, but strong in its completed form. We see this strength and stiffness in the Elizabeth Murphy House. As foundations have inevitably shifted by fractions of inches over the century, the Byrkit walls have moved together as if the main structural cube were floating.

During Mike Lilek's initial visit, the discovery of Byrkit lath in the basement and other places was another substantial piece of evidence that this home was designed by Wright.

But Byrkit by itself is not what created the strength in the walls. Sheathing would need proper aggregate to work. So Wright gave guidance to building contractors on materials to use:

> The interior plastering is to be of [brand name here] plaster mixed with 50% of wood pulp, or equal and approved brand of hard plaster. This plaster is to be applied in two coats, a brown coat and a finish coat.

And on the outside Wright directed the following:

> The exterior sheathing is to have a stucco finish which will be furnished and installed by the contractor. The material is to consist of [mixture here] which is waterproof, and is manufactured by the [company name here] or any other approved brand of water proofed exterior plaster.[4]

It is not surprising that a home built in the early twentieth century would contain asbestos as a fibrous binder in plaster, but Wright didn't call for the exact stucco mixture and didn't spell out asbestos as a filler. In fact, he left the selection of fillers used in the exterior surfaces to the builder. So where had Lilek gotten his suspicion?

In 2006, an American System-Built Home in Gary, Indiana, met a tragic end. It had lived a hard life, ending as a crack house and a foreclosure, but was purchased by an optimistic Wrightophile who thought he might restore it and turn it into a weekend rental.[5] The exterior was crumbling. When renovators found asbestos in the plaster under pebble dash, the demolition became a remediation, and then an unexplained fire gutted the house and cut the project short.[6] This sad story, available online, was public knowledge when we were shopping for our home, but as newcomers and amateurs, we had missed it. Anyone intimate with American System-Built Homes, however, including Mike Lilek, had taken note.

When the Burnham Block organization disassembled the Model B-1 to reassemble it as a tour stop, a forensic architectural archeologist named Nikolas Vakalis was employed to pull back the layers to look for and document clues about the program. He was charged with understanding original paint color and chemistry; the woods used in floors, cabinets, and trim; the sources of brick, sand, and pebbles; and the formulae for grout, concrete, and plaster materials to ensure veracious reconstructions. His report, on file at the Wisconsin Historical Society, declares unequivocally that 5 percent asbestos was found as a binding agent in the exterior stucco affixed to the Byrkit lath.[7] Interestingly, asbestos was not found in the interior plaster removed from B-1, suggesting a wisdom that only outside walls might require strengthening, since temperature change would be more extreme.

Before about 1920, when asbestos was not widely known to be the health hazard that it is known to be today, it was used for fireproofing, binding, and strength in many applications.

Today, residual asbestos anywhere in or on a home is a serious matter. However, when it is stable and undisturbed on the exterior, most experts will call it safe until nature or renovators begin to take it apart, releasing dangerous microscopic fibers into the air to be breathed and then to potentially cause asbestosis and mesothelioma.

We did not feel safe. Part of this home's exterior had become its interior when the open sleeping porch—with its pebble dash walls—was converted into a heated livable space that was now my office and our place for relaxing to read or watch a movie.

Admittedly, we were taken aback by the possibility that our new home might be historically priceless but also unlivable. How would we find the money to make it safe? Where would we live in the meantime? How could we give tours or socialize with friends when the first room they would see might harm them?

We sent samples to an accredited lab for redundant tests. They evaluated hunks of the plaster, a small section of wall including lath, stucco, and pebbles, and samples of dust taken from around the room.

Then we called the Frank Lloyd Wright Building Conservancy. In a worst-case scenario, we wanted to protect the artifact while ensuring the safety of friends, family, and visitors. John Waters, director of preservation, provided moral support and offered to call experts together to brainstorm solutions. We might, he said, find a way of encapsulating the fibers while leaving the historic specimen intact, but it would take time and specialized expertise and might hide a key curiosity.

Finally, the test results arrived.

Negative. No asbestos. A huge relief.

Herman Krause had left asbestos out of the exterior plaster that he applied over Byrkit lath sometime between 1917 and 1918. When the United States entered World War I on April 6, 1917 (the same month Krause started work on the Murphy House) the price for asbestos shot up because the military needed it for ships and other weaponry. We can deduce that Krause didn't have room to make up the higher cost in his fixed-bid contract or he might not have been able to get it all.

We can't know whether this was one of the changes that Murphy had wanted Wright to weigh in on. Ironically, as the specifications show, Wright would not have had an opinion on this specific question. It was serendipitous—to both the protection of the fragile artifact and our ability to share and live in it—that Frank Lloyd Wright had left the asbestos decision to Krause, the builder.

12

The Records

For a program that many people seemed to want to forget and only a few have written about, a vast trove of American System-Built Home records remain. Most were kept by the Frank Lloyd Wright Foundation until they were moved to Columbia University's Avery Library in New York City a few years ago. It is unclear whether this collection is exhaustive, but it is surely the most significant and complete sample. The collection is too large to digest in many days.

For example, the files contain drawings or a reference to at least 129 distinct American System-Built model designs (see accompanying table), though there were more models than the collection holds.[1] Not all models were built. Indeed, not all were even completely drawn. Some of the drawings are concept sketches, and others are renderings that could be used in advertisements or catalogs. Of the 973 drawings in the collection, 714 name a specific model home, duplex, or multifamily dwelling, and 259 are drawings that zoom into details not necessarily specific to a model—for example, window height options, a lineup of kitchen cabinets, or the dimensions of the galvanized iron tray that would line a flowerbox.

When a house was to be built, a package of construction drawings was created and a copy made for the contractor. The package for our model A203 includes the floor plan; the plans for foundation concrete, joists, rafters, roofs, pitches, windows, perspectives, doors, and walls; the location of built-in cabinets and shelves; the kitchen, bath, basement,

Summary of American System-Built Homes Drawings and Models

Descriptor	*Number*
Drawings dedicated to models	714
Drawings dedicated to common features	259
Models listed by number	129
Unnumbered drawings	40
Total model sets with more than one drawing	92
Total model sets with more than ten drawings	15
Total model sets with more than fifteen drawings	6
Drawings approved by Russell Williamson	151
Model sets approved by Russell Williamson	25
Drawings or models approved by someone other than Russell Williamson	0
Total drawings and models of various types	973

Source: Frank Lloyd Wright Foundation Archives collection, Museum of Modern Art, Avery Architectural and Fine Arts Library, Columbia University, New York.

and lighting layouts—most of the visuals necessary for the builder to make the house, with little left to imagination.

In the Avery collection, there are only fifteen models represented by more than ten drawings and only six of them by fifteen or more drawings. It is unclear just how many American System-Built Homes were built, but this collection offers clues, assuming that it is the substantial representative sample that it appears to be. It is believed that there are a dozen homes remaining from the twenty to thirty constructed.[2] Some models were built more than once, so quantity of model drawings loosely corresponds to built models if duplicates are subtracted.

Taken together, the collection suggests years of preparatory design thinking followed by a period of transition as ideas hardened into a program and then a flurry of activity as it was getting under way and being made commercial. Finally, we can see in the collection evidence of a quick yet painful death.

Before the program took shape and over some years, Frank Lloyd Wright had loosely assembled a family of concept designs for modest homes into a portfolio that he sometimes called American Houses and other times called "ready-cut." It seems to have begun more as a collection of thematically connected designs, not a system per se, but it would eventually evolve into one. Although the earliest drawings branded "American System-Built" homes share the date 1912, Shirley du Fresne McArthur saw work to standardize and mechanize small house design as early as 1901.[3] In fact, Wright had been using "New" together with "American" to describe a series of home designs with unusual (for the time) features—such as casement windows, banding, geometric brickwork, and built-in gardens—starting as early as the Lamp House, built in 1903 for his childhood friend Robie Lamp in Madison, Wisconsin.[4] The Lamp House is not an American System-Built Home, but Wright's idea to speak of it as "American" demonstrates a decades-long thread in his design vocabulary.

In late 1913, two years after Wright and Arthur L. Richards worked together at Lake Geneva and before the prototype Burnham project of six American System-Built designs was under way, Wright was assembling and shuffling a small team of draftspeople and assigning tasks to them to support the emerging project and to balance it with other studio work. The Avery collection contains renderings of one house called the "Small Town House," which was drawn many times, presumably by recruits vying for project work, including Russell Williamson. Williamson's rendition dates the design as created in 1912 and 1913. Since Williamson had been a student of architecture at Kansas State in 1912 and then took supplemental classes at the Art Institute of Chicago in 1913 and would not meet Wright until the fall of 1914, we can deduce that Wright had designed the Small Town House and then Williamson was asked to draw it when he applied for a job or soon thereafter. Williamson signed his name on his version of the drawing but didn't date it when he signed it. At least three other draftspeople created their own version of the Small Town House during this organizational period. Williamson's drawing shows characteristic style and precision: detailed shading, exact proportions and perspectives, and vegetation represented in outline.

The Small Town House, designed by Frank Lloyd Wright, signed by Russell Williamson, 1914. American System-Built (Ready-Cut) houses for The Richards Company, Urban House, View, Frank Lloyd Wright Foundation Archives, 1506.006.

Once Wright had the human resources in place to support his idea, the System was developed between 1914 and 1916. Richards's model Burnham Block project seems to energize this stage of the work and may have helped the team find things that worked and didn't work so that they could refine their ideas and methods. For example, some elements shown in drawings dated later in 1917 don't appear in the Burnham Block homes that had been built earlier, and some features found at the Burnham Block are not in later drawings and homes, indicating System evolution. Prototypes and their commercial progeny are never identical.

During Burnham Block construction, Russell Williamson earned the job of organizing designs and ideas into a family of models, though other draftspeople were involved and producing drawings.[5]

In late 1915 the studio was awash in creativity and the expectation that something big was about to happen. The team imagined and sketched entire neighborhoods of American System-Built Homes in promotional images, while also sorting out engineering details and planning placements of homes on lots on the same pages. These unofficial early works—like modern-day erasable whiteboards—are playful and free and evoke the spirit of optimistic and idyllic American urban places. The homes are elegant and open and the lots small. Two side-by-side homes are never the same. Doors and windows open toward the doors and

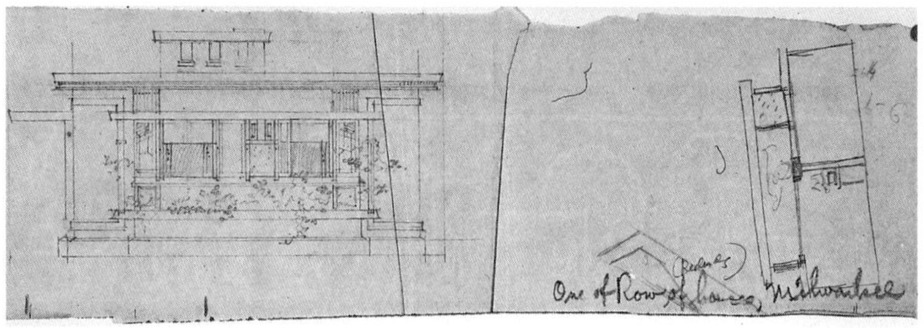

"One of Row of Houses" (the Model B-1 that would be built on the Burnham Block) noted by Russell Williamson. American System-Built (Ready-Cut) houses for The Richards Company, Elevation, Frank Lloyd Wright Foundation Archives, 1506.076.

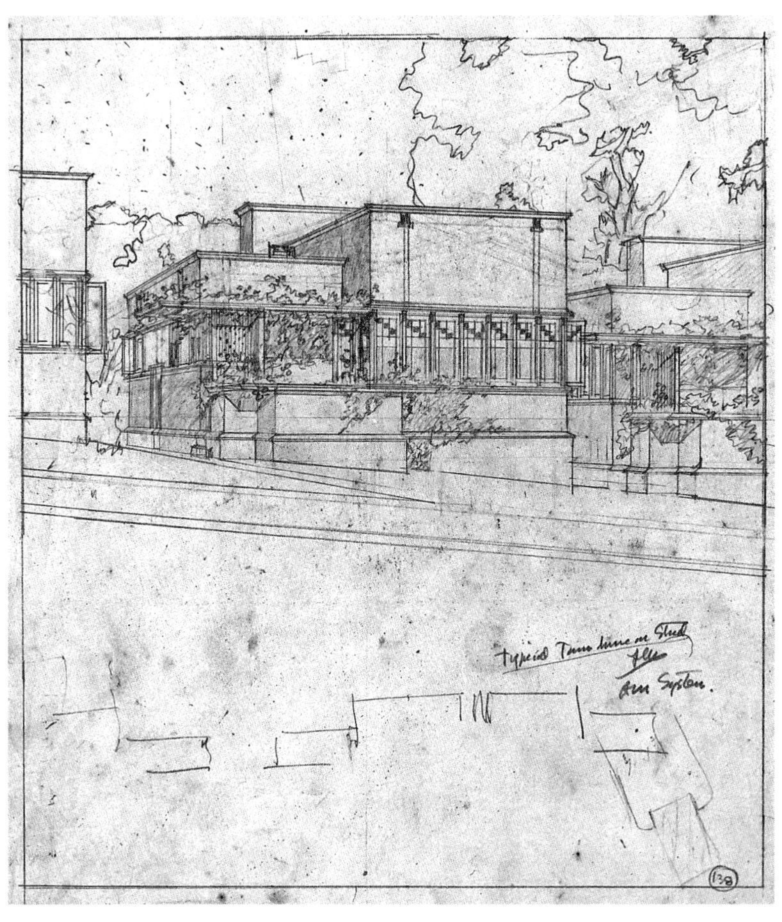

Model A101 in a row of American System-Built Homes, suggesting orientation and placements. American System-Built (Ready-Cut) houses for The Richards Company, View, Sketch, Frank Lloyd Wright Foundation Archives, 1506.056.

windows of neighbors. It is easy to imagine greetings from kitchens or porches, kids and toys spilling across yards, and neighbors shoveling snowy shared walks together.

Arthur Richards visited the studio often to participate in this creative effort, helping to make key decisions on matters such as the application of pebble dash stucco, which he called "stipples" and described in margin notes on a few pages as to be "light grey, medium and dark grey." *Stippling* is an artistic method of painting or drawing with dots. The pebbles in the pebble dash were to have a "stippled" appearance. Incidentally, three shades of gray pebbles—looking like dots from five feet away—can still be seen in our porch and in preserved sections of original exterior surfaces at other American System-Built Homes. On one tattered rendering, Richards wrote directions for the color of the stippling while Wright claimed ownership of the overall design by inscribing "F. L. WRIGHT ARCH., TALIESIN WISC" in pen and warning "infringers" in ink stamp that they would be held liable if they copied the design. The push and pull of the ownership of ideas is evident.

A ledger was created to list drawings and relationships between models. The ledger would include a page for each letter in a model series (A, B, or C) and a line for each model. Within this framework of letters and numbers, Wright organized ideas and choices that he deemed appropriate based on prior experience. In some cases, he recycled concepts from past work. For example, according to the historian Grant Carpenter Manson, Wright had presented a proposal in 1909 for a Prairie house design to be used to anchor an unbuilt subdivision called Waller Estates using three roof forms, "the early gable, the later deck and the perennial hip."[6] The American System-Built Model A201 was to have a flat roof pitched down and into a drain in the middle of the house. A Model A202 would feature a gable roof with gutters, and a Model A203 would have (as it does on the Elizabeth Murphy House) a hip roof, also with gutters. All versions would be built on the same footprint.[7] Three roof options were available on many designs.

Roof variation was one of many tools to *multiply* the architecture while retaining the System's DNA. For example, by offering three roof forms, a tract of land with space for twenty-one homes holding fifty

American System-Built Home rendering with handwritten notes by Frank Lloyd Wright and Arthur Richards. American System-Built (Ready-Cut) houses for The Richards Company, View, Frank Lloyd Wright Foundation Archives, 1506.105.

or more families might only require seven base designs and yet no building would appear like another. By mixing roofs on small and large single-family, two-family, and apartment units to assemble an American System-Built subdivision, owners and developers could create a neighborhood that would feel less like a row of blocks and more like a garden of coexistent and perhaps codependent species. Incidentally, this idea was lost on Arthur Richards when he selected only one duplex design—the model JC—to build four-in-a-row Burnham Block structures of the same model and roof form, varying only footprint by flipping one in mirror image.

Handwriting comparisons reveal that the ledger was organized by Williamson but that Wright provided most of the content. Williamson created the pages and numbered most models while Wright described the models in detail and made an inventory of available drawings for each. Richards also contributed during this phase, adding notes about model variations in the margins of associated perspective drawings, sometimes as the drawings were being entered into the ledger by Williamson. The collaboration had found a groove and its three main

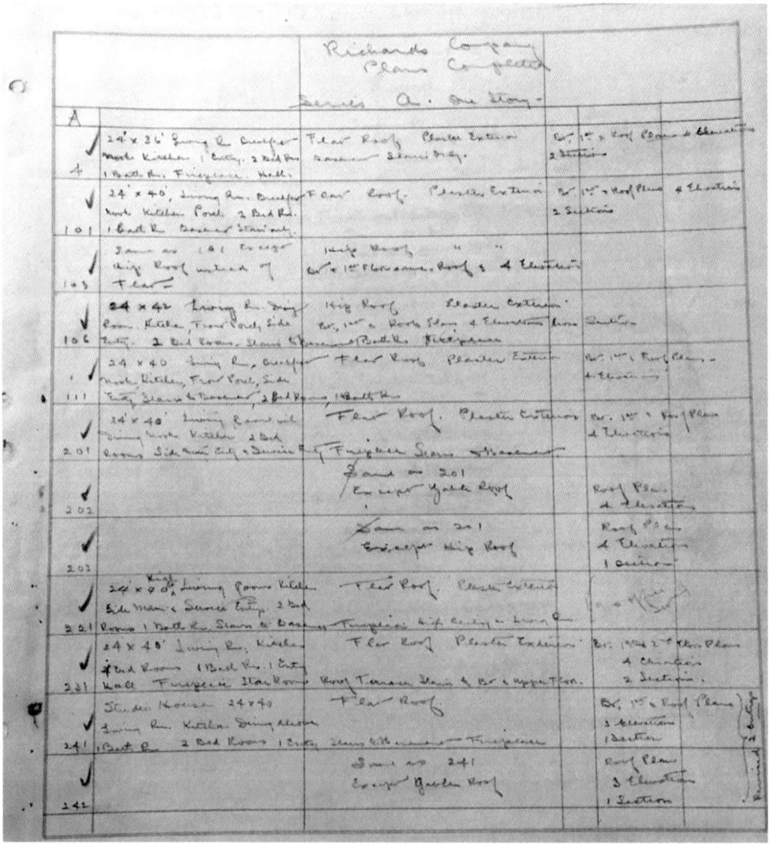

American System-Built Homes Model Ledger, page of A-series homes. Frank Lloyd Wright Foundation Archives, FLWFA Specs Box 2 1112–1903.

collaborators were riffing off each other. We imagine the occasional disagreement followed by compromise and laughter and cigarette smoke rising from the workspace as the lists, imagery, and possibilities grew. Under normal circumstances, a period of purposeful and energetic creative work like this would later be recalled by its collaborators as unforgettable and rare, a time when the edges of civility might fray but then come back into shape as camaraderie and pride. In this case, as we are seeing, these memories didn't last.

The creative work began to transition to outright systemization in early 1916. A vast library of instructional construction drawings would be required to support Richards's coming sales effort. If 129 models would eventually be built and each model required at least fifteen drawings, then almost two thousand construction drawings—plans, elevations, sections, plates, and details of roofs, rafters, joists, plumbing, attics, entrances and fireplaces—would be needed. This would be Williamson's main job for many months, though it might have seemed at the time like an effort that would last for years or even decades. The certainty of work and salary would be thrilling for someone just two years out of college and about to get married. (Russell Williamson and Nola Mae Hawthorne's wedding was held on May 20, 1916.)

Richards had hired an advertising agency called Taylor-Critchfield-Clague with offices in Chicago, Detroit, New York, and Boston to write copy and place ads and stories in newspapers, including the *Chicago Tribune*, the *Chicago Examiner*, and the *Milwaukee Journal*. He lined up a network of builders in Elmhurst, Berwyn, and other Chicago suburbs, as well as Gary, Indiana, and Champaign and Decatur, Illinois, and enlisted representatives who would sell throughout the region in return for commissions on sales. And he set up a supply chain to deliver lumber and materials to job sites.

To support this burgeoning network, on one day in May 1916, twenty-five sets (one home per set) totaling 151 working drawings were marked with a handwritten "OK," followed by Russell Williamson's first and last initials presumably as part of a hand off to Harold Richards, Arthur's younger brother who worked for the Richards Company in an operational role.[8] The complete text says "OK. RW. per [or for]

HAR 5/9/16" though it is often uncharacteristically hard to read, as if scrawled in ink hastily, page by page. Only one initialed drawing has a different date: 4/9/16. That appears to be a simple mistake because all corresponding pages read 5/9/16.

The Model A203—the design that would eventually become the Elizabeth Murphy House—is among the models with a complete set of working drawings with an OK from Russell Williamson and a handoff to Harold Richards in 1916. Not all fully drawn sets of other models were initialed. No other person did the initialing. Many of the designs seem never to have been approved and shared in this way.

Construction drawing detail is painstaking. Every section of wood is drawn with grain. Every milled dado, mortise, and tenon is shown to make the milling and fitting work simpler and the product beautiful. The geometries of wood for sills, rails, and molding are rarely square and often link together like polygon puzzle pieces. The dimensions of sheathing, the thickness of plaster, and the courses of brick are exact. Ridge shingles were to be cut on special angles to emphasize the peaks of a hip or gable roof.

There are also mistakes in the portfolio. A simple rectangular single-story house appears to be an outlier with twenty-five construction drawings, the most of any model. What made the modest model A106 special? The draftsperson—presumably Williamson—erred when assigning the

Russell Williamson's OK to transfer completed American System-Built House Model A203 to Harold A. Richards, dated May 9, 1916. American System-Built (Ready-Cut) houses for The Richards Company, Frank Lloyd Wright Foundation Archives, 1506.295 (detail).

same model number to both the gabled and hip roof versions, instead of designating roof-form with a sequential digit. The error was never corrected and the design unbuilt, as far as we know.

Finally, evidence of a last-ditch push to jump-start lagging sales and to save the program is seen in a July 1917 list of models with prices and single-sheet estimating forms that provided a manufacturer's base price for a model along with the material and labor costs of subcontracted work, such as lighting and carpeting. This work seems directed not toward prospective homeowners but toward dealers to help them understand the profit potential of a project. Moreover, instead of 129 models, this list contains only twenty-eight models, nearly an 80 percent reduction in choices. There are estimating forms for only twelve models, although individual pages may have been lost.

The items being promoted in the summer of 1917 with new sales tools were not necessarily the products that were ready for sale because drawings didn't exist yet or were not ready. Many models with price lists and estimating forms had not been included in the 1916 drawing package delivered to Harold Richards, and some model drawings seem not to have existed at all. These inconsistencies indicate a conflict between what was ready for sale, what the studio could support, and what may have been in demand from the dealer network.

From a dealers' perspective, the only saleable home was one that could be built, so despite the promise of new models and options, only models with a comprehensive set of construction drawings could be offered.

Notably, this vital package of dealer resources was created just *days* prior to Wright terminating the program and was probably made by Arthur Richards and his team, not Wright and his. If Williamson had a hand in writing with Richards, then the work would have been a great source of tension to the partnership. Wright had already decided that it was over. Should his assistant be spending time on it?

The System was stuck as a work in progress; a great architectural effort was still needed, and communication was spotty and strained.

In fact, real trouble had been brewing for months. A clue is found in a letter from Arthur Richards to Wright in February of 1917 reporting only one project under way, almost a year after the package of construction drawings was approved by Williamson and delivered to Harold Richards. Compounding the trouble, the war in Europe was intensifying and material prices were inflating.

The architectural historian Nicholas Olsberg wrote, "By the summer of 1917, they were trying to float stock to sustain the scheme."[9] Arthur Richards had missed obligatory payments to Wright and wasn't paying some suppliers, and he needed investors to help bridge the gap between the design and the sale of homes. Richards created a Delaware corporation with shares of stock to sell and transferred all the rights and contracts from his Wisconsin corporation to it. Richards did not tell Wright about the idea. Instead, he offered only a cryptic reference to it in his letter, saying that "we are working on a plan to get real money into it."[10] It is not clear whether the transfer was simply a matter of legal necessity, but when Wright realized what Richards had done, he found it threatening—evidence of an ongoing or upcoming theft. Therefore, subsequent legal filings by Wright's lawyers listed both the Milwaukee and Delaware corporations to track the whereabouts of and claw back Wright's intellectual property. Apparently, no investors were interested because no investments were made.

Building permits and sales records gathered by contemporary American System-Built homeowners suggest that Richards's last-ditch pitch to sell homes was at least modestly successful. At least three projects were started near Chicago and in Madison, Wisconsin, and drawings were supplied for a home to be built in Iowa in the summer of 1917.[11]

But it was too little, too late.

In total, the drawings and documents at the Avery Library reveal the evolution of an innovative, complex, interdependent system becoming a hopeful program organized over more than a year and then stopped on a dime. It took only thirteen months for Wright to hand over his initial portfolio of ideas, fully commit valuable studio resources to make them buildable, and then withdraw with a letter to Richards. The young Williamson, who was shouldering most of the work on Wright's System and having difficulty keeping up, would have been buffeted by the chaos that comes with shifting goals and, moreover, a boss saying one thing and a buyer saying another.

Wright was deliberate and intentional with his decision to stop the work and cancel the program. It is one of the first things that he did after returning from a four-month visit to Japan, and his termination letter was quickly followed by official legal action. He wanted the partnership and the projects to be done.

A personal note: To experience—to see and hold—the American System-Built drawings is to step briefly back to the early twentieth century, when industrial progress was creeping into and reshaping every American life, often for good but sometimes for bad. The production line and mechanized global transportation were hinting at the potential for widespread democratic upward mobility, but folks who had acquired generational skills to grow food on land were being pulled by economics and technology into cities to instead work on lines. Materials—hardy Cypress wood, for example—could be delivered long distances by train or river barge from Gulf Coast states to the Midwest. Yet, ink and pencil on linen paper were still the tools of skilled workers like Williamson who were fighting to earn skilled wages. A drawing copy was a copy made by a trained and talented person, not by a keyboard click. Wright's studios would feature bank safes to keep these valued works under lock and key. Still, builders worked from second-edition hand-copied prints—one degree removed from the original art. A change was made from a conversation about a problem needing solving, usually on the job site. And unskilled workers still used mules to carry rocks and dirt out of dug basements and to bring concrete, brick, and lumber to work sites. Architecture as a practice was just then learning to augment original artistry to find its role in the modern methods of building by proposing new systems. Good work depended on teams of architects to teach their new ideas to teams of sometimes skeptical builders. The bigger the project, the bigger the teams. The newer the idea, the more time and training required. The more distance, the more drawings, but even then, a perfect drawing might not result in a perfect outcome without direct interpretation. The ideas were too new.

I was overwhelmed by the magnitude and majesty in the designs, the care taken to ensure that they were executed well and the massive amount of detailed work done to create the System. Wright's spatial and geometric genius pops from every page. As I flipped through to look at one model and then the next, it seemed miraculous that one model could be as beautiful as the last and the next, yet also distinct—not just individual but *exotic* on its own merits while still connected in spirit. With every design based on a platform of common windows, doors, joists, cabinets, moldings, parts, and pieces fit into twenty-four-inch spaces, the portfolio seems almost da Vincian in its adherence to a fundamental geometric principle.

At the same time, the collection feels fragile, lonely and forgotten. How does one draftsperson review and approve 151 working drawings in one day? Why were there no more approvals after that day? Was there no one else to do the approving? Was there no more need to approve? Or were approvals happening outside of the chain of command?

13

The Unraveling

Daily life in the Elizabeth Murphy House is a paradox.

The spaces are serene. The lines are lovely. The proportions are perfect and the paths practical. The sun brings magic every day. You can get your work done, but only in between surprises. For example, as you go about a morning routine—pouring coffee, getting dressed, and making the bed—you are called to watch new sunlight march through the house, taking a different route than the day before. In spring and summer, the light is soft and glows floor to ceiling. But in the fall, when the low sun and oak leaves shift the spectrum toward orange, contrasts sharpen, colors pop, and the house feels and looks warmer. It is telling you that winter is near but all will be well. Can that have been planned?

At the same time, there are mistakes and shortcomings everywhere. Whereas Frank Lloyd Wright's plan was brilliant, Herman Krause's (and possibly Alfred and Gladys Kibbie's) interpretations, made under duress, were often either questionable or quirky.

For example, simple built-in bookshelves grace a wall near our fireplace. They are lovely and functional. Wright varied the shelf depths: a deeper section for bigger books that must lie flat merges into a shallower and longer section where the rest of the books in the small library stand on end. The cabinetry at the corners can only be called amateurish. Vertical boards are butt-jointed. Horizontal boards that form a crown combine miter joints next to butt joints, all within a few inches. On close inspection it looks more like a rough barn box than a quality cabinet.

We have learned to love these signs of one-hundred-year-old conflict and stress. There are many examples to love.

A basement railing post was an afterthought made from job site scraps: it mixes solid birch on two sides, birch plywood on one (a piece pillaged from the dining cabinet doors), and a scrap of cypress (a leftover from the outside trim) on the side that faces downstairs that guests won't see.[1] When you're running out of time and materials, you use what's on hand, and that is what happened here.

Unlike Wright's first home and studio in Oak Park, Illinois, which did not have electricity when it was built and required a wiring retrofit, every American System-Built Home would be wired and lit to start. Wright's plan called for "Simplex Chauch or Habershaw red cove rubber covered wire" and "Hart, Diamond H. or Arrow E. flush push button" switches to control ceiling lights. "Bracket lights" (today we call them sconces) with "chain pull switches at the fixtures" would eliminate the wire and labor to connect separate switches.[2] This house was to have eight bracket lights all fed by knob and tube wiring run through interior walls to prevent condensation, which would lower fire risk, and, again, speed the wiring during construction. Only one of these lights remains. In fact, it is possible that the fixtures that Wright would have suggested never made it into this house. A few American System-Built Homes still feature one or more bracket lights; a square five-by-five-inch plate with a 2½-inch cube containing a pull chain and socket into which a plain, clear incandescent bulb is screwed. In this home, scars in molding and plaster and remnant wiring visible in the basement show that Wright's lighting plan was not understood and therefore not executed correctly. First, the original sconces were round, not square, on the base. And although those sconces were located where the top-down floor plan drawings indicate they should be, they were not hung at the height that Wright wanted but instead were placed one foot higher on the wall, attached to the horizontal banding ringing the home. This suggests that the drawing package was not complete or that specific instructions didn't make it to the electrician finishing the work. The effect at night would have been to create high-contrast shadows and too little usable light where it was needed.

Unlike the crisp, simple rectangular scribe molding found in most other American System-Built homes and specified in the drawings, a Colonial molding connects banding to plaster in the Elizabeth Murphy House. There are thousands of linear feet of this out-of-place trim installed. We can see two possible ways that it was selected: Arthur Richards had not supplied the materials for the scribe molding, so Krause didn't install it and the Kibbies added it later, or Krause sidestepped the specification and bought what was available in birch at the local lumberyard to save one-third of the cost of materials not supplied. If this was Krause's doing, then he likely attached these boards while wondering whether he would be paid for them. We know now that he would not. Our guess is that if Wright had seen a Colonial molding in the house, he would have deemed it an outright travesty.

A bricklayer's interpretation of the grout work in between the bricks on the fireplace is haphazard. Wright's instruction that the bricks "shall be laid to a 3/8″ joint with the least possible vertical joint" is handled in two different ways despite only seventeen courses of brick on a four-by-four-foot mantel. Low courses near the floor that make the narrow pillars that bookend the firebox were laid three-eighths of an inch apart and filled with mortar that is not raked back from the surface, per the plan. However, bricks laid above the firebox were butted to each other, leaving no room for mortar. How did this happen? A clue is found in the construction of the hearth, which was to include a header but does not. Perhaps the material for the header was not included in the delivery of bricks, so the bricklayer began his work assuming one would eventually arrive, but when it did not, he changed methods partway up. His mistakes compounded: By beginning with half bricks at the base of both pillars instead of two halves on one side and a whole on the other, he was left with a wobbly transition between courses eleven and twelve, and by leaving out the vertical grout starting with course twelve, he subtracted almost two inches from the course length, requiring a nonstandard cut brick for one end of each remaining course.

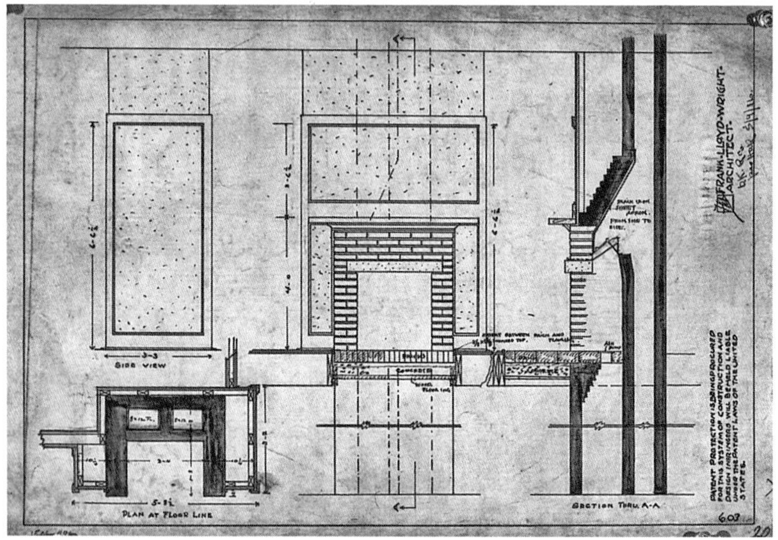

Fireplace detail. American System-Built (Ready-Cut) houses for The Richards Company, Basement Plan, Frank Lloyd Wright Foundation Archives, 1506.498.

Simple math says that if he had followed the drawing while still accounting for a missing header, the vertical seams would have lined up per plan and masonry common practices. Instead, you get the feeling that he just wanted to finish the project and go home.

The errors are dizzying; both types of vertical joints are technically deemphasized per Wright's plan, but because the technique and the seams shift two-thirds of the way up, your eye is drawn to the wrong thing. You find yourself studying the competition between architectural uniformity and interpretive masonry, and not Wright's emphasized horizontal lines.

Cabinet carpentry in the kitchen is also basic: butt joints and miter joints are held fast with nails; no glue. It's clear that as Krause was hurrying to make and install the upper kitchen cabinets just before walking off the job, he used the last imperfect scraps of birch to assemble the cabinet doors, leaving deep milling scars from Richards's lumberyard

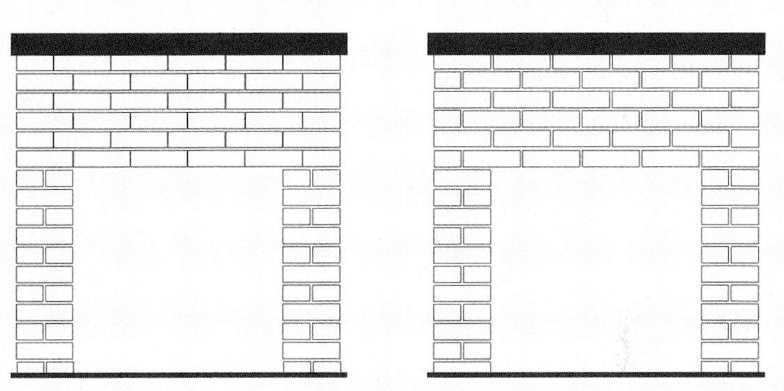

Fireplace as completed (*left*) and how it could have been built (*right*), despite the lack of a header. Image by Nicholas Hayes.

saw blade for all to see. The placement of one flawed board is perplexing. Instead of using it on a high rail of a cabinet door out of sight, it was placed at eye level on the most popular door to be opened: in front of the logical place for coffee cups and cereal bowls. We are, therefore, reminded of Krause's predicament daily. It is something a cabinetmaker would never do unless he wanted to make a point. The System wasn't working.

Since the Model A203 could alternately be purchased as a flat-roofed Model A201, an attic may or may not have been necessary. Therefore, an attic door was not shown on the original build drawings. However, since this house has a space between the ceiling and the roof, a door needed to be placed. Someone, perhaps Krause or a committee of workers, decided to locate it awkwardly on the inside wall of a small coat closet. To access the attic, the closet must be emptied, the shelves removed, and a ladder squeezed in, and then the person must climb and crawl through the tiny door like a spelunker. The attic contains nothing anyway because nothing can be reasonably put in it.

At the 2018 Annual Conference of the Frank Lloyd Wright Building Conservancy in Madison, Wisconsin, we presented some of the home's curiosities and had the opportunity to meet other owners of

American System-Built Homes to share notes. In our presentation, we showed pictures of the elegant shoe moldings that run at the base of every wall.

I had been working on touching up damaged sections of this fragile but beautiful shoe trim and blogging whenever I came upon new evidence that Richards's yard had supplied the lumber. Many sections of trim carry indicative markings. For example, "Richards Company—Milwaukee, Wis" is stamped on the wall-facing edge of one section of molding: the last *s* stamped backwards. On the underside of another section, a worker—presumably a lumberyard clerk—scratched the number of feet required for the whole house in blue crayon.[3]

After our presentation, we learned from other owners that the shoe moldings were installed in two ways, depending on the house and the contractor: with the long edge vertical or with the long edge attached to the floor.

American System-Built Homes in the Chicago area generally sport the long edge down.[4] By contrast, while visiting an American System-Built Model AA202 in Madison last fall, we noted that all shoe moldings in it are attached with the long edge up, as in our Elizabeth Murphy House. Subsequently, Michael Schreiber and Jason Loper, co-owners and stewards of the Delbert Meier House in Monona, Iowa, visited and reported shoe molding attached both ways, down upstairs and up downstairs.[5] So one goal during our visit to the Avery Library was to understand the original specification and reason for this detail and to try to explain these inconsistencies.

According to the drawings, the shoe trim was part number B-11 in the American System-Built part numbering system. No drawing in the Avery collection shows the trim installed with the long edge attached to the wall. Indeed, at least five drawings show it installed with the long edge down, as in the drawing reproduced here.

Inconsistent treatment of many elements—brick, trim, lighting—still visible in the remaining American System-Built Homes can be taken together as more evidence of trouble.

In a vacuum created by a sparsity of instruction passed from Wright, his support team, or the Richards Company, a subcontracting carpenter

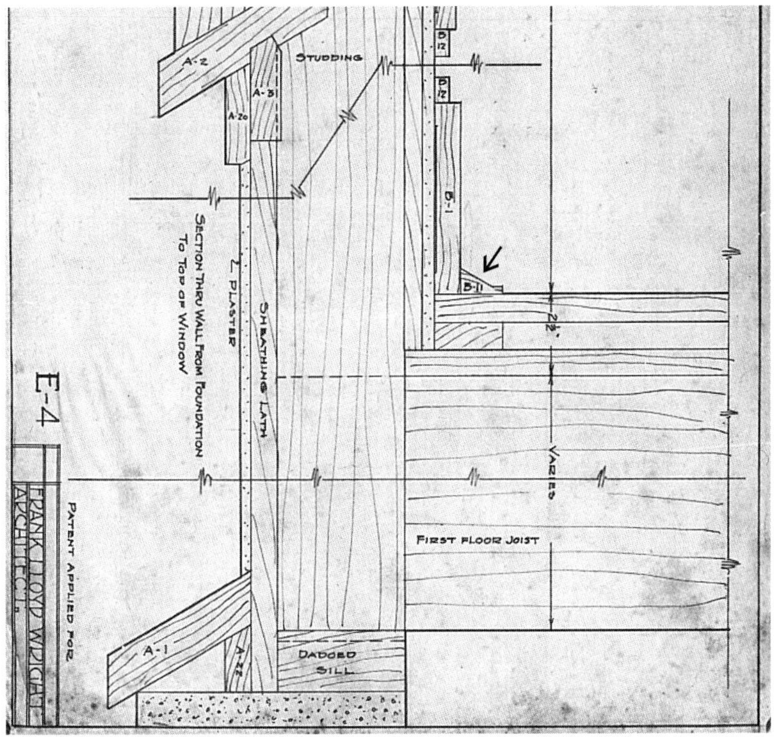

Shoe molding, part number B11 shown installed long edge down. American System-Built (Ready-Cut) houses for The Richards Company, Casements, Frank Lloyd Wright Foundation Archives, 1506.656.

could easily misinterpret the architect's intent and install as experience suggested. For example, none of the construction drawings for the A203 show the shoe molding orientation, so it is understandable that Krause or his crew would follow their intuition.

There is also evidence—in our saw-marked cabinets—that individual builders took it upon themselves to overrule the written or drawn instructions. To Wright, these would be serious flaws and, more important, infractions of contracts and agreements.

Finally, it seems that the System was not well coordinated. The drawing of details of our fireplace is strangely out of order in the Avery collection and lacks a model assignment, suggesting that it was not delivered in the portfolio to Krause. So the bricklayer punted.

We empathize with the craftspeople assembling these houses who were faced with these choices while working independently, on fixed contracts, with immense client expectations but nowhere to go with questions. Such is the risk of leaving some decisions to chance, and, more important, of creating an incomplete and unsupervised System.

The risk is palpable. We are reminded every day that it was a System that had quickly fallen out of control and, by the time it was handed to Krause to interpret the design into a dwelling, effectively didn't exist as a System at all. Still, Krause remained respectful of Wright's vision, given his lot.

Each time a newcomer visits, we experience the power of intentional design to engender and amass social capital. We witness spaces and places that Wright designed and Krause built forming friendships and trust among the people in them.

Recall that two narrow passages stand in the way of a first greeting by the hearth. To facilitate this sublime social exchange, Wright placed a three-quarter-height, six-foot-long dividing wall inside the front door, in order to direct people to each other. We watch as guests experience the transitions from space to space and are boxed by their journey into an authentic exchange at the Place of Greeting. Then, together, we replay the feelings and the fact that we have all just been directed to be clearheaded, cordial to, and empathetic with one another by none other than Frank Lloyd Wright. That Herman Krause took time and lumber to finish this wall, instead of omitting it as superfluous, is a living mystery and an experience that we wish for every friend.

14

The Exception

Frank Lloyd Wright unified his American System-Built Homes with branding, including elements made from two- to four-foot sections of vertical slats, like fences, that could be used as a partition or to indicate a door or window. Wright would call these features "light openings," though some of the drawings label them as "grills." The construction is similar to a narrow-slatted fence: a 1½-inch-wide vertical gap meets a 1½-inch-wide vertical wooden slat, followed by a gap, then a slat, and so on. Sections of light openings can be seen on the Burnham Block duplexes as staircase dividers and on single-family American System-Built Homes as partitions for terraces, sleeping porches, or entryways. The renovated Model B-1 in the Burnham Block neighborhood carries the element inside above the fireplace to screen a metal firebox that provides radiant heat into the main room. And although Wright designed only a few furniture pieces for the American System-Built portfolio, he carried the grill theme into the pedestal of a dining table and matching benches.

On the outside or in transition, the effect of a light opening is to create a small shelter—some privacy and shade—while allowing a breeze to flow between divided spaces. It is easy to see out of a light opening but hard to see in. Light penetrates, as the name would suggest, but in stripes that hit walls and floors as slow-moving abstractions of nature in the space.

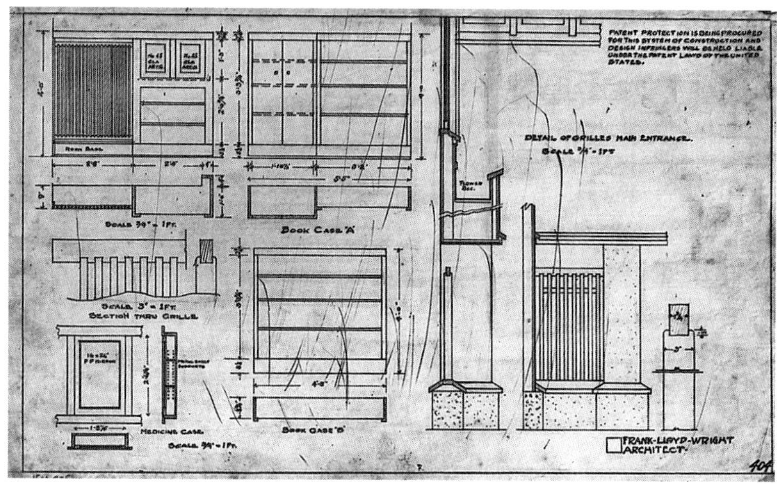

Frank Lloyd Wright's design for light openings, or "grills," on an American System-Built entryway. American System-Built (Ready-Cut) houses for The Richards Company, Grille at Front, Frank Lloyd Wright Foundation Archives, 1506.475.

Wright used this simple visual element as both a way to brand the program and also as a functional tool to improve the living experience of his occupants.

Wright's American System-Built Model A203 was to have had two sections of light openings, placed at one end of two of the half walls that surround the sleeping porch. Unfortunately, none of the planned light openings exist today on the Elizabeth Murphy House, and evidence suggests that they were never installed.

For example, Wright's drawings indicate an opening to the sleeping porch on the front wall of the house that would measure ten feet wide by four feet high. The opening would be divided asymmetrically, with eight feet completely clear of glass, screen, or beams, and two feet on the far left (as you face the house) decorated by a grilled light opening. Unlike the other sleeping porch openings, which were built to the exact dimensions on the original construction drawings, this front opening was built two feet too short—walled in where the grill would have been placed. It might seem that later additions such as siding could have covered up a grill, but the 1929 image and the preserved interior pebble dash rule that out.

Furthermore, on the east-facing wall opening, also now occupied by glass windows, there is no evidence of carpentry work to fill gaps where rails once were, and the cypress baseboards and headers are original and undisturbed. Grills were never installed on the Elizabeth Murphy House.[1]

As we have discussed, the sleeping porch was and still is both the most exotic feature of the house and its least practical. Since it served as both a patio and an entryway, it amounted to more than three hundred square feet of roofed but wet and cold space with meager daily duty and usefulness in its designed form.

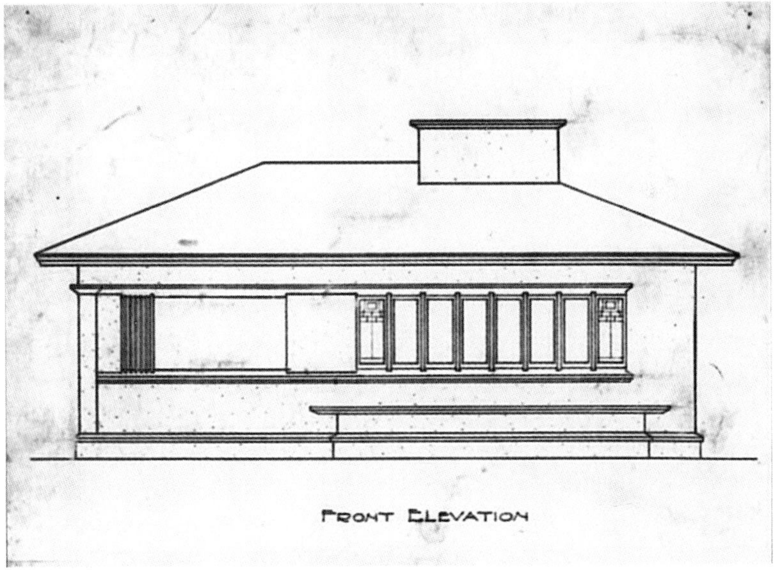

Front elevation showing light openings, or "grills," on the sleeping porch opening on a Model A203 (drawn in reverse of the home built at 2106 East Newton Avenue). American System-Built (Ready-Cut) houses for The Richards Company, Front/Rear Elevation, Frank Lloyd Wright Foundation Archives, 1506.295.

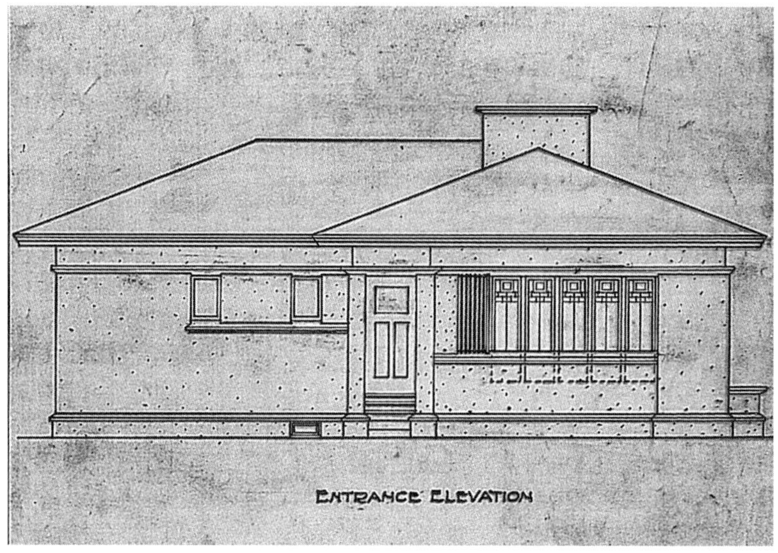

Side entrance elevation of the Model A203 (drawn in reverse of the home built at 2106 East Newton Avenue). American System-Built (Ready-Cut) houses for The Richards Company, Side/Front Elevations, Frank Lloyd Wright Foundation Archives, 1506.298.

That said, we can imagine a warm breeze blowing through it, with grids of sunlight and shadow crisscrossing the floor creating the feeling of a forest of tall pines on a summer day. It was another planned experience but one that has not been experienced by anyone, ever; an organic luxury drawn by Wright but missed by all because it was omitted.

The fact that the program's signature decorative feature was not included in this home forced us to wonder if the decision to leave out the light openings was made by the builder Herman Krause, the investor Elizabeth Murphy, or first owner-occupants Alfred and Gladys Kibbie. Given that the Kibbies could not have arrived on the scene until after the pebble dash was struck, we can eliminate them from our list of suspects, leaving the other two and leading us to surmise that either Krause had run out of money and lumber and didn't think that the light openings and the complex grid work to make them were necessary, or

Murphy made a speculator's decision to save cost and time on a tardy project and struck the luxury from the work order. In the latter line of thinking, it is easy to imagine that Murphy made the decision to enclose the sleeping porch so as to offer a larger home for sale, meaning that the grills were eliminated and the fragile pebble dash protected, though records of her decision don't exist.

The mishandling of light openings, among the myriad oddities in the building of the home, is the most visible change to the original specification, though it is not the most flagrant. The most flagrant change deserves a chapter of its own, to come.

A visitor once asked if we plan to return the sleeping porch to Wright's intended duty by removing the glass windows and adding, for the first time, these light openings. Unfortunately, we cannot. On the one hand, reopening the windows might bring the outside in again, but on the other hand, the historic pebble dash would then resume rapid deterioration with temperature change and be lost to the ages. So instead, this home must remain what it is: a Frank Lloyd Wright design that did not and will not boast Wright's most flamboyant branding, one that survived tumultuous times, kept its secrets well, and now is finding its own special place in history.

15

The Flip

Lawrence Murphy was a Milwaukee real estate attorney and loan broker. It is unclear how Lawrence acquired a parcel of land in what was then East Milwaukee, but records show that he transferred ownership of it to his wife Elizabeth via quitclaim deed around 1901.[1]

It also is unclear why it took the Murphys so long to build on the land or whether this was one of many parcels that they owned. It is clear that they were partners in investing. Lawrence deeded the parcel to his wife for estate, tax, or liability reasons, and after he did, she stepped into the legal, contractual, and management duties. She was the primary defendant and answerer on the later lawsuit filed by the builder Herman Krause, and she did her work skillfully: the case was decided in her favor.[2]

It is also unclear how Elizabeth Murphy acquired the drawings for Frank Lloyd Wright's Model A203 for her project. Perhaps she crossed paths with Arthur Richards in their real estate work and struck a deal. Although Milwaukee was growing fast, it was a relatively small market, and they may have been members of the same trade association.[3] Or perhaps they met on the sidewalk. The Murphys lived in what would become Shorewood, at what was then number 438 Edgewood Avenue, just four blocks from Elizabeth's investment parcel and where Richards's real estate work was active. Given their shared universe, they all saw profit in building or renovating and then *flipping* houses—that is,

STATE OF WISCONSIN,)
) ss.
MILWAUKEE COUNTY.)

Elizabeth Murphy, being first duly sworn, on oath says: That she is one of the defendants in the above entitled action; that she has read the foregoing answer, and knows the contents thereof; that the same is true to her knowledge, except as to those matters therein stated on information and belief, and that, as to those matters, she believes it to be true.

Elizabeth Murphy

Subscribed and sworn to before me
this ..eleventh..... day of November, 1919.

Ralph J. [illegible]

Notary Public, Milwaukee County, Wisconsin.

Elizabeth Murphy's signature on the Answer of Defendant, Case Number 56124, State of Wisconsin, Milwaukee County Circuit Court. Courtesy of Milwaukee County Historical Society.

quickly reselling them at a higher price. Elizabeth, Lawrence, and Arthur were speculators.

In fact, the Murphys and Arthur Richards had stakes in parcels of land on the *same* East Milwaukee block on which they would build homes to sell. The Murphys owned the plot on the Newton Avenue side of the block where they would build this house by Wright, and Richards, via one of his real estate companies, would invest in at least two plots on the Beverly Road side of the block, only two hundred feet away, facing in the opposite direction.

This is a clue we will return to later. For now, it bears repeating and elaboration: When Shorewood had fewer than five hundred homes and was being subdivided into narrow lots that would contain tightly spaced homes, the Murphys owned lot six of block 1 in the Hillcrest

Village at 440 Newton Avenue. Meanwhile, Arthur Richards bought lot numbers 8 and 9 on the north side of the same block, at 427 and 429 Beverly Road, the next street north. The lots are back-to-back and only three and four doors apart. The block straddles a gentle hill, which would have had few if any trees in 1917. It had been recently cleared as farmland and then subdivided to make a village. Laborers erecting houses on the small block could share jokes and stories or toss a ball during lunch breaks without leaving the rooftops of the houses on which they were working. By 1919, all three lots had houses on them.

Speculation was an activity that Richards, a self-described all-around "real estate man," actively pursued and promoted. A newspaper advertisement from 1909 boasted that the Richards Company was involved in forty projects in many Milwaukee suburbs, with many lots ready for building homes and others with "ready" homes on them. Richards was a wide-ranging real estate entrepreneur. He could fluidly act as agent, builder, banker, buyer, and seller, and he would create business after business throughout his life to segregate and handle the work.

His experience had shown that speculation might energize the marketing of the American System-Built Home program and, in the near term, would be a source of immediate sales and cash flows. In conversation with potential dealers in new cities, he would suggest that the best local billboard would be the building and then the flipping of a model American System-Built Home. Some dealers agreed. The Model AA202 in Madison, Wisconsin, was a 1917 speculation by a construction company vying to earn a place as an American System-Built contractor. The A. B. Groves Building Company bought the lot and built the home with intent to sell it at a profit, while showing it to others in the neighborhood along the way.[4] The Guy C. Smith House in Beverly, Illinois, was built speculatively by a local representative, according to its current owners, Debra and David Nemeth.[5]

Richards and his publicists prepared marketing materials for customers that he called "Men Planning to Build Subdivisions," promising buildings at a fixed price with no surprises: "You buy the house, erect it and can deliver [it] complete, key in hand, ready for your customer to live in."[6] What better way to help an impatient American into a finished home? Moreover, with a lot and a fixed-price contract, what better way to see predictable returns on investment if you dabbled or dealt in real estate?

Richards, like Wright, had seen persistent American impatience but, unlike Wright, thought it should be *exploited* and used to increase business and profits. It was what a speculator would do and how he would engage with others doing the same.

Meanwhile, Wright deemed the practice of speculation a cancer to his craft and antithetical to his goal of affordability. In one of his most quoted pieces of the time, "In the Cause of Architecture," published in the *Architectural Record* in 1914, Wright complained:

> Personally, I too am heartily sick of being commercialized and traded in and upon; but *most of all* I dread seeing the types I have worked with so long and patiently, drifting toward *speculative* builders.

He worried that speculators were preying on and profiting from American impatience and was concerned that his own apprentices might not be able to resist the draw of the predictable flow of work and, in that work, agree to sacrifice quality for speed and volume. He observed that the profit motive drove a "cheapening" that resulted in the "robbing of quality and distinction."[7]

Complicating matters, Wright had agreed to a contract with a dealer (Richards) who would sign other dealers to reach distant markets of real estate developers and speculators. Ironically, the American System-Built program would quickly confirm his suspicion that any system that lowers costs might just as easily be exploited by those same real estate developers seeking quick returns. This is not to say that Wright did not see the need for businesses to succeed. Instead, he could see that another man's version of success might conflict with and hinder his own ability to meet goals. Said simply, Wright's American System-Built Home vision was to promise Americans of modest means a decent-quality, distinguished home at a reasonable price. Richards's American System-Built Home vision was to promise dealers and developers, like Elizabeth Murphy, a predictable and quick return on investment. Our timeline suggests that Wright agreed to test the waters—to dabble in rapid, widespread urban development—but almost immediately recognized that it was not for him. Efficiencies can be used in progressive ways or profiteering ways, but seldom both.

Serendipitously, Wright sensed quickly that his System was in trouble, in part because of these stacked layers and competing motives but also owing to the impractical physical distance between himself and Richards. He could not course-correct from Japan.

On January 1, 1917, just one month after Wright had arrived in Japan, Richards made an urgent plea for help, targeting Wright's baser needs for financial security and fine objects with a handwritten note sent via international mail. In cursive, ignoring periods and commas and with the emphasis of stream of consciousness, Richards scratched:

> Do not worry if we do not send you money to buy Japanese prints believe me every minute of your time is needed here you can make more money making plans you must work close with us this year and your financial worries will be over we are in sight of the goal don't think anything but the system.[8]

It is not clear if or when Wright replied. Absence of a reply in the records of correspondence suggests that he did not.

Hearing nothing, and perhaps wishing to take some words back, Richards reframed his message in a typewritten, single-spaced two-page report to Wright on February 6, 1917. He began by sharing progress made in signing dealers and subdealers. He talked about focusing time and effort in Cook County, Illinois, where relationships seemed to indicate that homes would be ordered and then other more lucrative work might emerge, such as an apartment complex on Chicago's wealthy North Shore. He discussed problem personalities in the dealer network and shared plans to address them. He acknowledged Wright's wish—perhaps a mutual goal—that the work should be attractive to capable people and talked at length about the team that was working on the project. He seemed to be proud that a culture of competency was forming around the System and believed that this was what Wright would want.

He reported that "Stanley Clague is giving us more time continuously," noting that Clague had been granted shares to make him a minor partner and that recognition seemed to spark effort. He summarized that project members Clague, Spindler, Pettit, and Rockwell were "able, competent, active men." He made specific mention of Russell Williamson, whom Wright had left in charge of his Milwaukee projects, reporting that "Russell Williamson is developing into a very strong man and works well."[9]

However, he also complained, with a gentle hand, about Wright's limited and incomplete contribution and extreme remoteness:

> The other big work that we have had to get under control, was in getting out the plans of the sketches that you left, and in getting our work detailed, ready to offer our dealers. This, of course, I appreciate you did not think was much work, but the completed plan I find,—the plan as we must have it 98% perfect, in fact should be 100% perfect for the field men, is no small task, and when that end is perfect Frank, just that minute AMERICAN SYSTEM-BUILT HOUSES will be enormous financial success.[10]

Richards was making clear that in order to offer limited or no supervision for contractors, there *must* be exact instructions for those contractors to follow and that Wright's System was neither complete nor exact.

And he was calling for a direct solution: he needed Wright's time and creativity in Chicago, not Japan. Williamson could not do it alone. In fact, plan production had ceased completely when Wright left the country and Williamson was sent to Milwaukee to supervise.

From Wright's perspective, the economics and practicalities could not work. A few small house commissions could not justify the massive job of finishing a flexible yet scalable System. Most of all, Richards was asking Wright to divert time and energy away from the Japanese emperor, on the assumption that men like Herman Krause would follow Wright's instructions to the letter. It was an impossible ask: that Wright should choose against a lucrative artistic commission—with all the trappings of fame, fortune, prestige, and elite company—to return to Chicago to instruct anonymous builders to make anonymous houses for anonymous dealers selling to anonymous people. There was no fame, no fortune, no prestige, no elite company in that.

These letters put Wright over the edge. They made clear that the concepts of affordable strength, beauty, production efficiency, and client experience that made up his System, as conceptually elegant and flexible as they were, had devolved without him and turned to work against his values. He had relinquished design control on the bet that volume would be self-sustaining and the hope that quality would not suffer, but instead his choice had created chaos and confusion that would result in substandard products. From Wright's perspective, Richards's proposed solution was to shift more of the work to the architect while devaluing the architecture. This he could not do—not with a sparse project ledger, not from Japan, and not from his heart.

Richards may have thought his letters would buy time and secure a deeper commitment from Wright. Ironically, by sending them, he forced Wright's hand and simultaneously gave Wright the out that he needed. Within weeks, Wright returned from Japan, checked his bank accounts, noted two months of missed payments and incomplete accounting, canceled the program, sued for back pay, and didn't speak of the American System-Built Homes again.

Historians such as Shirley du Fresne McArthur have had to conclude that Wright's decision to end the program was based mainly on slowing housing starts due to the war and then postwar inflation. However, if this had simply been a matter of poor timing, why didn't Wright postpone instead of cancel and cover up the work? He might have set his plans to the side and rereleased them when demand resumed. We see that there is more to the story, a fundamental problem evidenced by the improper shoe molding, milling marks, and old newspapers found in our tiny house: the System had unraveled. Wright had neither the time nor the will to fix it. Most important, he and his partner had competing visions about what America could and should be, and how to get there. The art was now tarnished.

Here is where the deeper omission begins. Wright made a stark but strategic choice. He would claim the time and space—postpone the idea of bringing organic design to the common man and woman—for another day and on different terms. Indeed, it would take two decades before he would try again. The dust needed to settle. The players needed to part ways. Reputations needed repair. Memories had to be cleared to be rewritten.

PART THREE

How to Build an Architectural Legacy

16

The Miss

Russell Barr Williamson saved no records. Apart from the many buildings that he designed, details of his architectural work and daily interactions can only be pieced together from memories, correspondence that mentions him, a few articles he wrote, and a few that were written about him. Whereas hundreds of books about Wright have been published, we could find no commercially published books about Williamson. Almost four decades after his 1964 death, his son and granddaughter painstakingly assembled a record of his career, along with notes and comments from friends and former clients. The work was self-published in 2000 by an entity called "The Barr Brand." A few ring-bound copies can be found in libraries in Wisconsin. Although the authors admit to not knowing where all of Williamson's work happened, they took care to create a comprehensive list of projects and reflected as a proud family would on a successful fifty-year career and a life well spent. The house at 2106 East Newton Avenue is not on their list.[1] Their research relied heavily on research done by Juanita Ellias thirty years prior.

In the early 1970s, Ellias was a student working on a master's degree in art history at the University of Wisconsin–Milwaukee. She was intrigued by many Prairie-style homes from the 1920s sprinkled throughout Milwaukee and nearby suburbs—few attributed to Wright and many rumored to have been designed by Williamson—and she undertook a research project to shed light on their true origins. Ellias saw that historians of the Prairie style had altogether missed or omitted Williamson as a contributor to it. She wanted to correct their oversight, arguing that Williamson's work had "transformed the Prairie Style into an economically viable one."[2]

Ellias attempted to solve the riddle of Williamson's time with Wright. She asked Williamson's family about it and found frustration with their father's unexplained unwillingness to discuss the relationship and work.[3] Williamson's children could not get him to talk about Frank Lloyd Wright. Ellias knew that the period had been formative—that was apparent in Williamson's style—but was left with more questions than answers:

> There are many questions concerning Williamson's years with Wright. Such questions, moreover, are complicated by the uncertainty surrounding Wright's work and activities during this decade. Thus, when we ask—when did Williamson join Wright?, where did he work?, how was he trained?, what projects did he work on?, when did he leave?, and why did he leave?—we can only outline the questions and, in most instances, only indicate the problem and point to the more reasonable answers.[4]

Ellias could not conclude, for example, that Williamson had worked exclusively in Chicago for Wright or whether Williamson had spent some or any time at Taliesin.[5] She could not say exactly when Williamson started and when he stopped working for Wright and why. Most important, she could only speculate, using interpretations of style and drawing techniques, about which work was Williamson's, which work was done by another draftsperson, and which work was done by Wright himself.

Throughout her research, she ran into barriers and gaps and sought workarounds—ways to sidestep those barriers—while still fairly representing the inconsistencies in the Williamson story. For example, in a late-life interview conducted by David Link, a reporter for the *Milwaukee Sentinel*, Williamson could only recall working on the Imperial Hotel project while working for Wright, claiming to have supervised all of the architectural planning for it.[6] Historians at the Frank Lloyd

Wright Foundation told Ellias that this was flat-out impossible, insisting that all of the supervisory work was executed in Japan by Japanese draftsmen. Ellias did not dispute the foundation's firm position, deciding instead to overlook Williamson's claims and focus on what was clear and apparent in the records that she could find.

Williamson had not been helpful; he made no mention of any other effort undertaken while at Wright's studio, including the development of the System. However, Ellias found Williamson's fingerprints all over the American System-Built Home program. She found him named in Arthur Richards's writing and in the accounts of work done on the Munkwitz project. She found Williamson's handwriting on forms and lists, his drawing style on countless images, and his name penciled on one of the test renderings of the Small Town House design created, presumably, by Wright's apprentices and assistants petitioning to do the work on the American System-Built project. She didn't ask the question explicitly but seemed to wonder why Williamson would omit the experience—obviously a large and long-term effort—from his memory and personal history.

Despite Williamson's desire to hide his work on the American System-Built Homes, Ellias pursued it. She uncovered personal connections between Arthur R. Munkwitz, Frederic C. Bogk, and Arthur L. Richards and the work completed at the Burnham Block and the Munkwitz Apartments. With these insights, Ellias was able to account for much of what was happening in and around Milwaukee in the period between 1916 and 1917, when Williamson was working here and, for at least some of the time, acting as local architectural interpreter and supervisor on behalf of Wright.

Furthermore, she saw Williamson's subsequent independent career springing up from his work on the System and in this neighborhood. She found many Williamson-designed homes built in the area beginning in about 1921, after Williamson had left or was let go by Wright and when Williamson had returned to Milwaukee from Kansas City to start his own practice, starting with many new projects for Richards. She studied resemblances in Williamson's work to Wright's. Some Williamson designs descend from the Bogk House; Williamson's own house looks a lot like Wright's Allen House in Wichita, Kansas, a commission from 1916 completed in 1918. She noted similarities between Wright's "fireproof" house and Williamson's "square" house and found other homes that are close cousins to American System-Built models.

She visited these homes, interviewed owners and the Williamson family, charted the course of projects, and described an evolution in Williamson's designs. She observed that he began building houses that would be easily confused by amateurs as attributable to Wright, while adding statement features, such as symbolic Greek columns framing the Prairie front door on his own house in nearby Whitefish Bay. He would then dabble in bungalows and two-family duplexes and more classic steep-pitched roof designs. Eventually Williamson would assemble an eclectic portfolio, though Ellias found one key theme persisting: throughout his career, she noted, he created methods of standardization to speed and automate job site work. With this observation, she proposed that Williamson had been charged by Wright to develop some or many of the processes that would underpin the System in the American System-Built Homes. Wright had sketched the System as a framework and directed Williamson—who had the organizational propensity—to fill in the details.

Ellias cited Wright's own words about his style of teaching to support her suggestion:

> I assign to each [apprentice] a project which has been carefully conceived in my own mind, which he accepts as a specific work. He follows its subsequent development through all its phases in drawing role and field, meeting with the client himself on occasions, gaining an all-round development impossible otherwise, and ensuring an enthusiasm and a grasp of details decidedly to the best interest of the client.[7]

There was historic context to support Ellias's supposition that Wright challenged Williamson to apply mass production techniques. Prairie-style architects and housing developers had been trying to marry the low-slung forms with the high-volume opportunity of suburbs for at least a decade, and Wright's plan for American System-Built

Homes would build on that trend. In his 1958 book *Frank Lloyd Wright to 1910*, Grant Carpenter Manson wrote that Wright's earlier "Hoyt and Hunt houses are inexpensive buildings whose *parti* is the simple cube, the cheapest to erect and maintain. It was an inevitable scheme if the Prairie House was to be reduced to the economic level of popular housing."[8] (The Hoyt House was built in 1906 and the Hunt House in 1907.) Wright asked the young Williamson to take up the cause and assigned early American System-Built work as test cases on which his assistant could learn and build. As witness to the experimental Burnham Block and supervisor at the Munkwitz site and working closely with Richards, Williamson was well positioned to see and write about ways to streamline work and parts, ways that could be deemed best practices and enforced procedurally later. Here again we confront, as Ellias did, the ambiguity of attribution. Whose system was it? Is any system comprehensive? That is, can it account for all variables on day one? Or does a system mutate as new environmental factors become known and new actors join the crew? Who then owns the mutations?

Amazingly, in 194 pages of meticulous study and reporting, Ellias completely missed Wright's American System-Built Home Model A203 while conducting her research from a university campus only five blocks from the Elizabeth Murphy House, walking in and around its neighborhoods and visiting the 2100 block of Newton Avenue to stand directly in front of the house to take pictures. She committed pages to the interpretation of the Eggers Bungalow across the street at 2101 East Newton, noting its similarities to the Bogk House. She also identified Williamson-designed homes at 2301 East Newton, 2308 East Menlo Boulevard (one street south), and a duplex at 3705–3707 North Maryland Avenue, three doors away and around the corner.

With Williamson's unofficial biography and Ellias's mostly unimpeachable local research, we created a map of Williamson's work done in close temporal and geographic proximity to the Elizabeth Murphy House. It paints a neighborhood drama or, perhaps better said, a culture of whispers, canards, and gossip. When Shorewood was a small village of three or four thousand neighbors, and during the same years that the Kibbies were regretting and covering up, completing, and not inviting friends into their embarrassing Frank Lloyd Wright–designed cottage, *eleven* Russell Barr Williamson commissions were being built within five blocks! By 1929, more than twenty families were raising children in at least seventeen Williamson houses in young Shorewood. Kibbie daughters Mary and Teddy would attend school with those kids. Dorothy Hoffman recalled a high school history teacher once talking about a nearby home by "that famous" architect. Teddy would not raise her hand to claim it as her home. Dorothy assumed that the teacher was referencing Wright, but classmates other than Teddy may have thought the famous architect to be Williamson because many of them lived in one of his homes. If the Kibbies had hoped to keep up with the Joneses, they could not; the Joneses had picked Williamson as their favorite architect.

Williamson had become a local celebrity and socialite. Dorothy recalled Williamson frequently visiting her childhood home. They lived blocks from each other, and he had befriended her parents. She described a jovial, charismatic man carrying a cane and wearing a long coat and a fedora, and who liked to consume ample amounts of her dad's pizza and beer. She was impressed that he had a lot of money, or at least it seemed that he did.[9]

Williamson had earned this celebrity in the long shadow of the Kibbies' inadequate home and their complex relationship with it and its architect. While supervising the construction of his Eggers Bungalow in 1921, Williamson watched from the walk as Gladys and Alfred Kibbie planted shrubs to cover the flowerbox and hung awnings to cover their windows, and as plumbers delivered and installed the fixtures necessary for American suburban living but that had not yet been installed in their American suburban home. In fact, Williamson spent years in silent witness to the Kibbies' discontent and the burden of Wright's brand on their daily life.

It is hard to imagine how Juanita Ellias, standing on the same walk as Russell Barr Williamson fifty years before, might have missed the Elizabeth Murphy House and its significance despite its clumsy exterior cover-ups. The garage, its most glaring and confusing modification, was not here when she walked by, so the house was less disturbed and more obviously a Prairie design with Japanese influence. The main windows, exterior trim, and flowerbox were exactly the same as those seen on the American System-Built Munkwitz Apartments, which were still standing at the time and important to her study. Two of the front windowpanes still featured an American System-Built motif in their leadwork, though awnings may have shrouded the intricate detail.

Ellias explained in conversation that with graduation approaching and a paper focused on Williamson's entire career, she could only list known American System-Built homes in an appendix and a search for unattributed homes was left for others. Whether she had a hunch about this house or not, she didn't have the time to express it. If not for missing a slightly premature though vital clue, hidden in plain sight, Ellias might have connected the dots to prevent the forgetting of this home in the first place.

Researchers work to uncover new information on top of what is known to confirm or correct the record. Knowing what is known was far more difficult before the networked computer and digitized text made ideas available and instantly searchable online. Ellias had to walk, read, and knock on doors. Her research had been extensive to the degree that was possible at the time; she visited the Frank Lloyd Foundation to see all of the archives from Wright's studio and projects during Williamson's time there, including the American System-Built drawings and documents. She searched the public record for the permits and deeds from the places where the men worked and then visited the sites. In July 1972, however, just as she was kicking off her primary research, a sunny bungalow at 2106 East Newton—"designed by Frank Lloyd Wright"—was listed for sale in the classified ads of the *Milwaukee Journal*. It was the third time the home would be offered for sale, each time with its famous architect named as a key selling point. Ellias didn't see the ad, perhaps because it was printed during summer break or maybe because her research was in its infancy or the main themes of her thesis were still forming. The house was quickly sold and changed hands in early September 1972, and she turned in her report in the spring of 1974.[10] It was a near miss that has rippled through art and architectural history. Had Ellias seen the ad or, more directly, had the new owners stepped out onto the walk to share what they knew about the heritage of their home as she was snapping pictures of Williamson's Eggers Bungalow in 1973, the historic record would have been more complete.[11] Shirley du Fresne McArthur would have had far more American System-Built history to explain. Richard Johnson would not have stopped to ring Pat Wisialowski's doorbell but instead would have only slowed his MG to admire and take a snapshot. Mike Lilek would not have had to visit the basement at 2106 East Newton Avenue for the world to know about this home by Frank Lloyd Wright. This story would not be new, nor this book necessary, because Ellias would have found more answers than questions about the time, and the work done during it, that Wright and Williamson shared but both wanted others to miss. The dark years would be less dark.

The cover-ups on this house by its owners and makers had succeeded in covering up history. It would take forty more years for the Elizabeth Murphy House to emerge and for the house to finally reveal what it was that needed to be covered up.

17

The Overlap

Herman Krause intended to finish Elizabeth Murphy's house in four months. It was a reasonable estimate for a small frame dwelling, and American System-Built Homes were designed and promoted to be built quickly. According to Murphy's answer to Krause's lawsuit, "said building was to be completed within four months from the date of said agreement, that is to say, not later than the seventeenth day of July 1917, but that said building was not actually completed until about July, 1919."[1]

What would a delay from four months to twenty-eight months look like? An excavation in the earth that rain and snow turn into a muddy mess needing to be reexcavated over and over? Supplies by the wagon-load sitting unpacked for months on the front walk? The frame of the house standing unfinished and skeletal for a winter or more? Pictures have not been found, but neighbors must have watched and wondered. Krause, Murphy, and Wright must have been the subject of ugly gossip.

A key question: How much of the mess did Russell Barr Williamson witness and what did he report to Wright?

Shirley du Fresne McArthur's research found that Arthur Richards's business records were lost in 1955. He never married and had no children. Items of perceived value were given to a youth foundation, but files and papers were carried away by garbage collectors.[2] Many of Wright's records had been lost in the Taliesin fire in 1925. Williamson's wife Nola Mae told interviewers that Williamson had destroyed his old records.[3] Since no contracts and correspondence with and about Williamson during this time remain, historians such as Juanita Ellias have been hamstrung to explain his exit from Wright's employ.

A clear picture emerges from the Elizabeth Murphy House.

We know that construction on Murphy's lot began in April 1917 and that Williamson was in the neighborhood at the start and stayed until sometime in the fall of 1917 as foundations were dug.[4]

It was during these months that a deviant, defiant, and definitive decision was made. Elizabeth Murphy's answer to the Krause lawsuit in 1919 reflects that "the plaintiff did not construct or cause to be constructed a concrete basement for said building, as required by said agreement, but that instead he caused to be constructed a cement block basement for said building."[5]

Indeed, the home still stands firmly on cement block, not poured concrete.

Frank Lloyd Wright, however, was explicit about the materials and techniques to be used to build the foundations of American System-Built Homes:

> Cement is to be Universal, Wolverine, Atlas, Marquette or any other approved standard brand of Portland Cement. The concrete is to be mixed in proportion of one part Portland Cement, three parts torpedo or coarse sand, and five parts gravel or crushed rock, ranging from ½″ to 1″ in diameter, and is to contain enough water to make the mixture sufficiently wet so as to obtain a smooth uniform finish. No tamping of concrete is required. Concrete is to be placed so wet that tamping will not be necessary.

To ensure proper setting, structural integrity, and a good finish, the forms were to be "accurately constructed to conform with the drawings and constructed tight enough to contain concrete." All exposed surfaces were to be "smooth and true" when the forms were removed.[6]

Wright's experience with and commitment to concrete as a creative and flexible architectural platform spanned his career, from the wondrous slab-sided Unity Temple in 1905 to his textile block homes built in the Los Angeles area in the 1920s to the flowing and fluid Guggenheim Museum, which opened after his death in 1959. At the time of the American System-Built Homes, the creative and constructive use of concrete was being improved and streamlined by powerful new combustion-driven machines that could dig and mix and pour quickly. It was just the kind of modern innovation that Wright would favor. In fact, the Wrightophile historian Richard Johnson's sleuthing focused narrowly on homes with poured concrete foundations built between 1915 and 1930 because he saw the use of concrete to make basements and to support homes as transitional and therefore as solid evidence of Wrightian influence.[7]

Hence, the care taken to specify the mix and the construction methods for concrete indicates that the materials and processes were elemental to the System.

In late May 1917—when excavation work was complete and forms were *not* placed in the hole to receive a pour, but masons instead began stacking cement blocks—Elizabeth Murphy's house was already seriously out of spec and destined for delay. Krause likely had placed the first courses before the change was noticed. Murphy probably questioned the decision with Krause and then Richards, and work stopped for a time. Richards would have looked to Williamson. The young Williamson would have hesitated at first and then either argued with Krause and lost or willingly approved the change without Wright's approval. Neither decision would have gone over well with Wright.

Notably, in her answer to the Krause lawsuit, Murphy insisted that construction or design changes were to be approved *only* by the architect Frank Lloyd Wright, and by exclusion, *not* by Williamson. Murphy saw a leadership vacuum swirling around her project—a gap or a shortfall in local authority—that had put her investment at risk. Williamson had been hanging around but lacked jurisdiction. Richards seemed more worried about the program and his other nearby speculations than her house. Indeed, by explicitly naming Wright as the keeper of changes, she reveals a deep concern about changes approved, or at least overlooked, by others, including Williamson and Richards.

She was right to be concerned.

Mike Lilek's research turned up time-stamped evidence of the chaos that resulted from this stoppage: a lien agreed to by Arthur Richards to the Landeck Lumber Company for not paying for "certain lumber and merchandise . . . for and delivered at a building erected for Elizabeth Murphy by a contractor named Herman Krause."[8] The lien was issued on June 4, 1917. Within weeks of starting, Krause had stopped work, awaiting an answer on whether his brick would be allowed. Murphy was holding payment to Krause, so Krause was holding payment to Richards, and Richards was holding payment to the lumber yard. And, it should be noted, this also was the time when Richards was missing obligatory payments to Wright. The project was in deep trouble as soon as it began, and the young Williamson faced severe pressure from Richards and Krause to accept the cinder block change. Still, Murphy wondered if cinder block would do, given that Wright—her architect—was explicit that her home be set on poured concrete.

Meanwhile, in April 1917 Wright returned from a four-month visit to Japan, the same month that construction started on the Elizabeth Murphy House, and while he had much on his plate, he dedicated a good portion of his time to reevaluating the American System-Built program. He was not pleased with what he saw. Sales reports from Richards had stopped, but drawing demands continued. Richards had moved his assets from Wisconsin to Delaware, presumably to raise capital, but possibly, Wright thought, to hide accounts and copies of ideas and drawings. Drafting work had stopped because his main project draftsperson was in the field supporting builders. Wright wasn't being paid what was contractually due, though he was paying the salary of a man to work full-time alongside his nonpaying partner.

But did Wright know about the Murphy fiasco?

Williamson seems not to have been forthcoming about the troubled project. If he had reported on conditions at 2106 East Newton Avenue to Wright as they were happening, then Wright's rationale to cancel the program becomes clear and our story is near its end.

Instead, we see a larger drama unfolding: secrets kept, uncovered, and then hidden again.

Within a few months after returning from Japan, Wright drafted a letter to Richards to terminate the contract and projects and to return all drawings for the American System-Built Homes program. A draft of the letter, on file at the Avery Museum, is not dated, was not legally binding, and appears to have been unsent. Instead, the letter was improved—perhaps with counsel from Wright's lawyer Emerson Ela—to be legally assertive. Wright was organizing for a fight and deciding who was on his side. In the letter delivered on August 11, 1917, to Richards's Milwaukee offices Wright alleged:

> Your company has made such use of the inventions, plans, details and specifications furnished and provided by the undersigned as to violate the provisions for the execution of the buildings according to the intent and the meaning of the said plans and specifications.
>
> Such buildings stand as an injury to the professional record of the undersigned, and furthermore, the plan of operation of your company assures no responsibility on its part to the house owner or to the undersigned as architect, that the plans and specifications will not miscarry,—except a merely nominal one of no real effect.[9]

Here Wright reveals that he knew about ongoing projects, that changes were being made on the fly, and that Richards was not preventing them and in fact may have been promoting them. From Wright's perspective this was a breach of contract and a risk to the architect and the homeowner. From Richards's perspective, Wright's instructions were not clear enough to enforce, so he created room for interpretation, with Williamson as his shield.

Meanwhile, cinder blocks had been anchoring the Murphy House for months, and Krause was battling other material shortages, cost overruns, and unclear instructions, all necessitating architectural decisions that Wright would not make and Williamson was never supposed to make.

With Wright's command to cease and desist in August, Williamson could no longer support an American System-Built project like Murphy's either officially or unofficially. After allowing the foundation to be built of cinder block, he had to go silent.

Furthermore, Williamson could see that after the Murphy project, few new Milwaukee projects would follow. Wright's reputation wasn't gaining in the neighborhoods where Williamson was working. The war and Wright's indiscretions, distance, and distraction had caused a decline in new business that would force hands. Williamson knew that he would not last as an employee and should be preparing for his next career move. If, in the summer of 1917, Krause or Murphy had complained again to Richards, and Richards to Williamson, or if Krause had complained directly to Williamson, then Williamson quietly chose Richards's side and said nothing to Wright. This, he would later realize, would define his relationship with Wright, the arc of his career, and his place in architectural history.

Within weeks of Williamson's last day under Wright's employ, Wright's stern letter to Richards had become a full-fledged lawsuit against Richards's Milwaukee and Delaware corporations for past due commissions.

The case reads as a straightforward but serious business contractual dispute. Wright alleged that Richards was in breach of contract for non-payment and claimed damages. He claimed that Richards was planning to keep his drawings and sell and modify them without his permission. Richards hired his own attorney, answering the lawsuit by denying intent to steal designs and then counterclaiming that Wright was in breach of contract for failing to deliver adequate plans and instructions. An injunction was granted by the court allowing houses started before August 11, 1917, to be completed. Along the way, Richards fired his attorneys and was not represented at (nor did he attend) court hearings. He seems to have given up. In the end, the court ruled against Richards and ordered all drawings and documents to be returned to Wright, and Richards paid the judgment.[10] However, having just sold a handful of projects in the last months of the agreement, Richards had been able to limit some of his financial exposure.

Wright was also concerned about exposure, but of a different kind. Emerson Ela had entered into evidence a letter that he received from Wright in preparation for legal action that opens a window into Wright's forlorn relationship with the program and its players. It was handwritten in ink on both sides of a piece of studio-branded Japanese linen, and it began:

> My Dear Mr. Ela,
>
> Richards—as might be expected has complied only to make a bluff at it.
>
> The following is lacking and he retains copies of everything he returns of course. We should insist on the total disappearance from his office or his agents of all copies of plans or any advertising matter.

Wright went on to provide a detailed inventory of drawings that he was sure that Richards still secretly possessed. For example, he listed:

- D303 3 Story Front Porch, Hip Roof, Balcony, Maids Room
- A.4 Isometric Plans
- A 101 24″ × 40″
- A 221 24″ × 40″ High Windows on Front
- A 231 24″ × 40″ 2 Story Roof Garden
- A 243 Interior Perspective

and *twenty-seven* other models.[11]

Wright's careful, comprehensive reconstruction of inventory and intellectual property reveals his state-of-mind. He was deeply and personally invested in the designs and in the American System-Built program, and he was afraid, hurt, and angry that his ideas might be lost or stolen. He knew his System inside and out. He knew the models by their numbers and the features by their application. It was a brilliant System built on a lifetime of thematic design thinking and he loved every part of it. He didn't want it to be taken from him, but more important, he didn't want it to be weakened or compromised in any way. His System could not be allowed to become a caricature of his original vision.

And then Wright lamented to Ela:

> *They* have so hacked up the plans in the work that they [the plans] are practically worthless.

Who was "They"?

Certainly Wright blamed Arthur Richards and his brother and partner Harold Richards. Downstream, contractors like Krause were taking liberties without Wright's permission. But the blame for having "hacked up the plans" can only have fallen to Williamson, who had prepared all of the delivered drawings and instructions, handed off the first batch to Harold Richards, and then worked side by side with Arthur Richards's team and their contractors every day, cooperating, collaborating, debating, and approving changes he shouldn't have approved, ignoring others, and not reporting on them. Moreover, Wright had concluded that copies of drawings kept by Richards as part of his bluff had to have been made by Williamson, in whom he had invested and pinned his project hopes. Williamson's loyalty had shifted to the men in Milwaukee and away from Wright, and Wright knew it.

There is no record of a final conversation between Wright and Williamson.

Mysteriously, Wright's handwritten note includes its own perplexing omission. Instead of submitting a complete sheet of studio stationery as Exhibit 2, someone, perhaps Ela, tore away a three-by-three-inch square from the corner just below Wright's signature. Whereas the main body of the letter delivers a complete thought and gives Ela the ammunition he needed to win the case, it appears from this crude redaction that Wright had something else to say and that Ela deemed it legally irrelevant or risky.

Had Wright written a slanderous postscript? Was this his first and only written mention of Russell Williamson? Or did someone simply need a scrap of paper for another purpose? Some omissions keep their secrets better than others.

Regardless, Williamson would be glad that he was gone from the studio in the fall of 1917, for the wrath of Wright was surely upon him. And he wouldn't have to worry about Elizabeth Murphy and Herman

Krause anymore, because he hastily retreated to Kansas City for all of 1918 and part of 1919. He would let the dust settle in Shorewood.

Finally, Williamson's lifelong silence about the house at 2106 East Newton Avenue is the most conspicuous of all the omissions we have discussed so far.

That he knew of it can't be disputed. That he didn't talk of it suggests a simple scenario.

Although there isn't a formal record, their silence suggests that Williamson and Arthur Richards shook hands in a gentlemen's agreement to not mention Elizabeth Murphy's project again. Since the Kibbies would not care one way or the other and could be trusted to remain quiet too, silence would preserve local reputations until they might be improved. Given the lawsuit between Wright and Richards and the tiny dimensions of the Murphy fiasco in the context of Wright's other problems and work, Wright would not care either. We can't be certain whether Richards ever mentioned the Murphy project again, but Williamson seems to have taken the commitment to his grave.

In fact, their accord rightly predicted Wright's silence too. They didn't need his handshake. Wright had his own plan to be quiet. Indeed, he would omit much more than one house from his records and memory, and he would not need the other two men to do that.

Wright's letter to his attorney Ela concluded:

> The only thing of any value in this situation is to stop them absolutely and clean up all traces of relationship between the Richards Company and Frank Lloyd Wright so far as is humanly possible.[12]

18

The Pickup

On October 12, 1919, an advertisement appeared in the *Milwaukee Journal* for a "bungalow erected on your lot" by the new company American Renaissance Inc., which promised, "By our system of construction of and manufacturing of the parts of our houses we are able to guarantee the quality of workmanship and materials." It further urged, "You will be greatly surprised to see how reasonable are our prices on various completed AMERICAN HOUSES."

A demonstrator Model Number A533 was available for inspection at 427 Beverly Road and would be offered for sale with a lot "47×120."

The house would come up for sale ninety-seven years later in 2016 and was still listed for sale in 2017. This time, the advertisement would say "Frank Lloyd Wright conceived American System designed home w/ Architect Russell Barr Williamson."[1]

Given that the house is 250 feet behind our American System-Built Home, we had to have a look. Serendipitously, on the day of the open house, we arrived five minutes after Mike Lilek, the expert on American System-Built Homes who had confirmed the authenticity of our own. We smiled and greeted each other with nods on the front step.

The seller described a rich history and connection with Frank Lloyd Wright; all technically true. Richards's letter to Wright extolling the good work of Williamson and making his second urgent plea for faster and more copious drawing production had been tacked onto an easel as evidence.

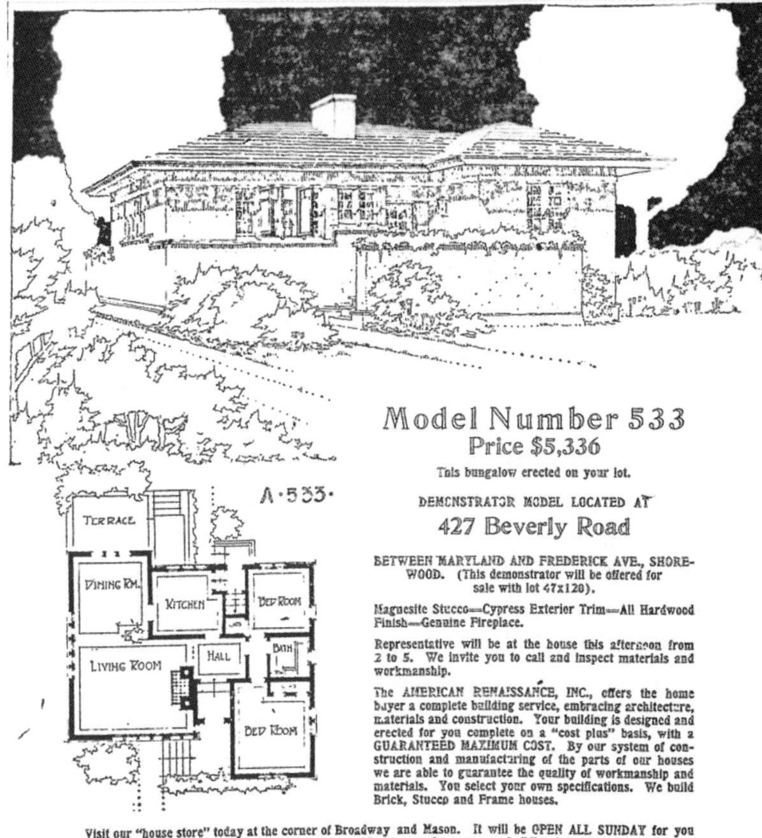

American Renaissance Inc. Model Number A533, offered by Arthur Richards, designed and drawn by Russell Barr Williamson, as advertised in *Milwaukee Journal*, October 12, 1919.

The asking price was high for a house its size and condition, the seller said, due to its pedigree. "Another American System-Built Home had sold recently just around the block."

Wright's words "Personally, I too am heartily sick of being commercialized and traded in and upon" popped into my head, though that may have been unfair. The history was spotty. The man was doing his job.

"We're aware of it, yes," I said.

The Beverly house four doors down and behind the Elizabeth Murphy House had long been rumored to be either an American System-Built Home or a close cousin. It shares the angled exterior banding and long overhangs. The roof pitch is similar.

William Allin Storrer, author of *The Architecture of Frank Lloyd Wright, A Complete Catalog*, had wondered about the home and considered it to be a possible suspect.[2] Burnham Block docents had been heard speaking of a "possible American System-Built Home" in Shorewood near the Model A203.

Lilek was cordial but visibly impatient. He wanted to see the basement. We followed him down. In just five minutes, Mike concluded that the house could not be an American System-Built Home. He pointed to the two-by-ten-inch floor joists spaced sixteen inches apart. (Recall from chapter 10 that, in an American System-Built Home designed by Frank Lloyd Wright with his geometric and organic principles, they would be two-by-twelve-inch joists spaced twenty-four inches apart.)

For us, the house had become another odd artifact in the mystery of our lost home, another contemporaneous Prairie design just a stone's throw away. We needed to know more about Williamson's role in the Model Number A533.

Juanita Ellias had studied the Beverly house too. She listed it as one of the "Houses Built by the Richards Real Estate Company After Designs Provided by Williamson(?)" in her thesis and included a copy of another *Milwaukee Journal* advertisement listing the home for sale in 1922, this time by the Richards Real Estate Co.[3] The house had not sold under the American Renaissance brand but was transferred to another of Arthur Richards's real estate holding companies and then relisted.

Shorewood Bungalow for sale by Richards Real Estate Co., as advertised in *Milwaukee Journal*, February 19, 1922.

Ellias was correct in suggesting that the home was designed by Williamson but was incorrect in dating the home as completed in 1922. She had missed the earlier 1919 advertisement. The Williamson family book would also list the house as one designed by Russell but built in 1922, one year after his Eggers Bungalow. Shirley du Fresne McArthur also found the 1922 advertisement for the prototype bungalow but missed the 1919 advertisement. Everyone's dates were incorrect, perhaps because subsequent researchers all relied on Ellias's earlier work, which had proven to be exhaustive to the degree that anyone could have known at that time.

Despite the end of the American System-Built Homes project in 1917, Richards had purchased and was still holding real estate plots on which to build houses and would need help with design and a system to build them. Williamson—educated, eager, privy to Richards's methods, knowledgeable about the System, and no longer with Wright—would be Richards's logical choice for the work. Richards and Williamson saw legal room in which to maneuver; Williamson knew about Wright's claims in patent applications and could avoid infringement by adjusting details, and neither Williamson nor Richards were bound by a nondisclosure agreement or a noncompete clause.

However, to legally work in Wisconsin, Williamson would need a state architect's license. In 1919, he wrote to the licensing board:

> Should you desire reference as [to] my ability and character, I would suggest you communicate with the following persons:
>
> Arthur H. Helder, Landscape Architect,
> Reliance Building, Kansas City
> H. J. Waters, Editor, Kansas City Star
> Maurice Herbert, Architect, Oak Park
> Frederick Bogk, Alderman, Milwaukee,
> Arthur L. Richards, Milwaukee.[4]

Despite almost four years of working for Frank Lloyd Wright, Williamson left Wright's name off the reference list that he included with his architectural license application. It might have seemed that to omit Wright would be to sidestep risk, given Wright's tarnished reputation at the time and because Williamson's and Richards's reputations and legal and local prospects were also at stake, due in large part to the Murphy fiasco. The paper trail needed cutting. Given their plans to pursue a derivative of system-built houses, it would be better not to mention Wright as long as there were angry customers in the neighborhood, especially coming on the heels of a lawsuit canceling the original System-Built program and legally assigning the ideas to Wright. The omission also betrays Williamson's emotional baggage after having been fired by Wright or forced to leave Wright's studio unceremoniously. He did not want Wright to enjoy any credit for his making.

Richards and Williamson would not waste a minute picking up the pieces of the American System-Built Home project to rebrand and restructure it with their own ideas. With complete architectural control, Williamson would take radical surgical steps to make the System his own: instead of Wright's twenty-four-inch balloon framing scheme, Williamson would specify that American Renaissance Homes be built using the more common sixteen-inch distance between studs. It may not have saved wood, but it was faster and more familiar, lowering complexity and guesswork for builders. Quick, on-time construction carried more weight than aesthetics.

Williamson's American Renaissance Model Number A533 seems to be the progeny of Wright's American System-Built Home Model B-7.[5] By comparison, a Model B-7 would have been 1,088 square feet, and the Model A533 is 1,044 square feet. The main bedroom in the Model A533 is larger, a front terrace is removed and replaced with a half-walled

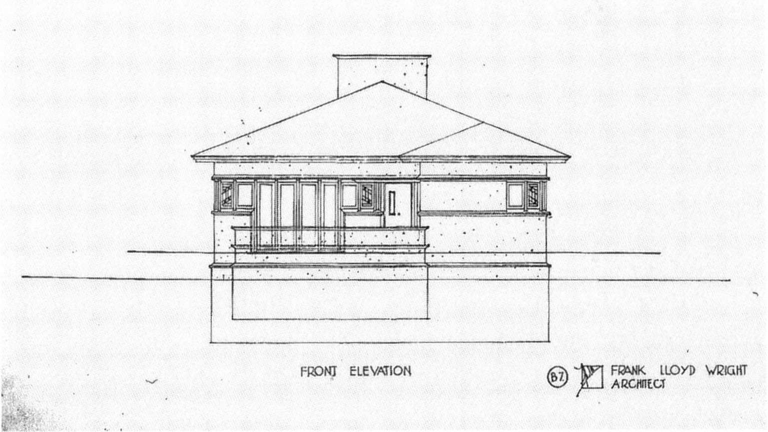

Wright-designed American System-Built Model B-7, a likely progenitor of the American Renaissance Inc. Model A533. American System-Built (Ready-Cut) houses for The Richards Company, Front Elevation, Frank Lloyd Wright Foundation Archives, 1506.871.

walkway, and the main hall is walled and doored, demoting the open hall to a closed passage and cutting off interior sight lines. Williamson would specify cement block to make the foundation for the model home rather than the poured concrete as Wright would have required.

Another key difference between the two models is their windows. Because Williamson's interpretation would need headers to support walls with the factory-made windows that remained in Richards's lumberyard stock, he would move his windows to places that Wright would not—into small groups or singles in the centers of walls. Headers at corners would be difficult and expensive to assemble, and so corners with a 270-degree view were ruled out. Wright called for thirty-five windows in his Model B-7, wrapping every corner and sometimes bathing entire walls end to end in light. Williamson's adaptation has only twenty-five windows, a nearly 30 percent reduction in light and visibility. The effect is a more conventional cottage with smaller, darker interior spaces rippling throughout the rest of the design. There would be no garden experience from the bedroom. There would be no large social space. There would be no path of discovery, no compression and release, no Place of Greeting. Guests would be met in a foyer at the front of the house and enter a hall with a uniform ceiling height. It is not clear whether there had been an organic motif in art glass in some of the windowpanes, but drawings suggest not. There are no shadow-making light openings (grills) or garden overhangs. And Williamson would shift the fireplace from the middle to the front of the house and shrink the chimney from an oversized "belvedere" to a simple brick stack.[6] Japanese influence had given way to what might now be called "ranch" styling.

Williamson and Richards had kept some of the factory assembly and job site efficiencies that were promised in the American System-Built project but sacrificed most of the organic experiences that Wright had designed. On the surface, this would seem like good business. It would be easier—and take fewer instructions and detailed drawings—to tell a carpenter contractor to build a wall using common methods and measures like studs placed sixteen inches apart, and then to add windows in the middle of the wall and not at the corners. After all, Shorewood was a destination neighborhood; someone would buy the house no matter how many windows it had or where they were placed.

The system was officially Americanized.

The house did not sell for three years, and during the long wait Richards had a change of heart. He dropped the American Renaissance brand and offered the home instead as a Richards Real Estate Company bungalow. Why? Richards was still walking a tightrope. The Dane County Circuit Court had ruled that all drawings and specifications, the "American System-Built Houses," and the "American System of Construction" were the exclusive invention and property of Frank Lloyd Wright and that Richards had no rights to use or sell the ideas "perpetually thereafter."[7]

Moreover, slow sales convinced Richards that the marketing of a "system" of buildings might never pay dividends. Speculators would appreciate the promise of a machine-built dwelling, but the same message heard by a prospective owner raised suspicions of poor quality. Richards—and by inference, Williamson—had learned that systematization is better kept as a quiet instrument of profit and not a buyer benefit, so the last breath of any American System was exhaled here.[8] Meanwhile, Wright, as we know, had moved on.

In fact, in what appears to be a parallel but divergent experiment on the plot next door, Richards built a home in the Tudor style, also to be sold as a completed property. The side-by-side houses are opposites in style and form, except for similar window casings and identical foundational cypress trim, undoubtedly from Richards's lumberyard. It is unclear whether Williamson was the designer of the Tudor home, though there is evidence that he might have been. The Tudor is positioned on the lot so that the front door is on the side, and Williamson is known to have designed at least two nearby Tudor style homes a few years later.[9] These clues suggest that he had some say.

We dug again into our timeline to see what else could be seen. This time, we focused on what was happening when the Murphy House construction project was unraveling and up to the point when the Model A533 was advertised.

Working back from October 12, 1919, when the Beverly house was listed as available for inspection and accounting for both a very short four

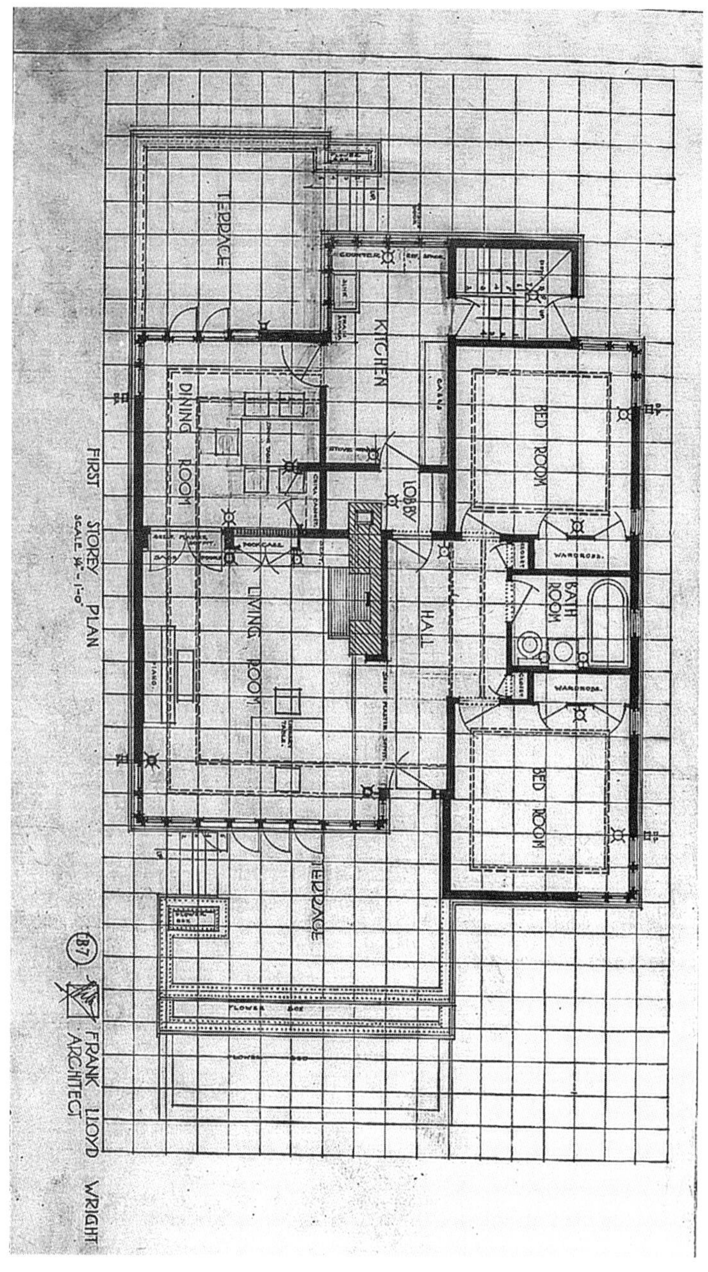

Wright-designed American System-Built Model B-7 floor plan.
American System-Built (Ready-Cut) houses for The Richards Company,
First Floor Plan, Frank Lloyd Wright Foundation Archives, 1506.870.

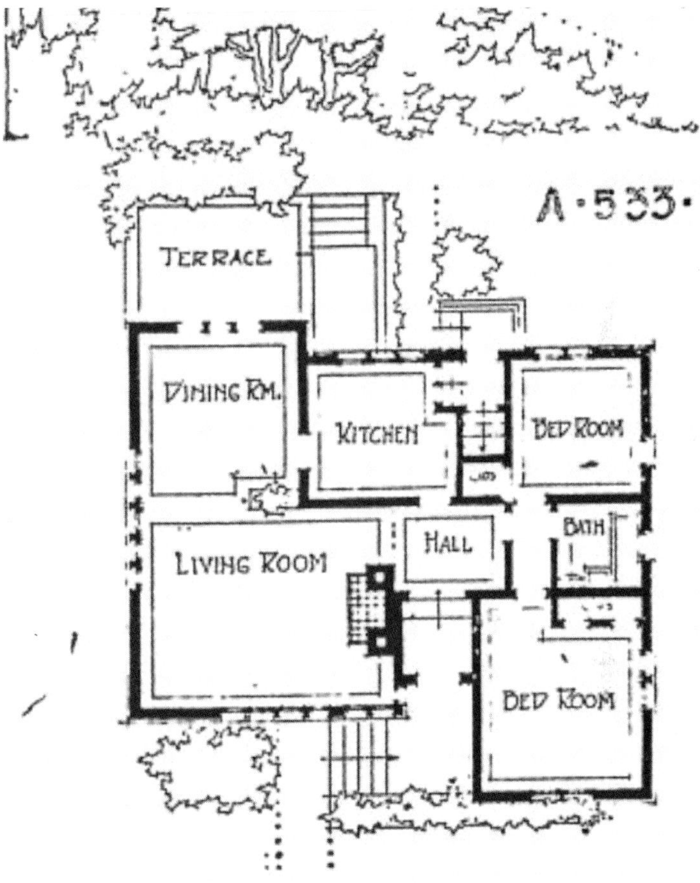

Floor plan of Russell Barr Williamson's American Renaissance Inc. Model A533, as advertised in *Milwaukee Journal*, October 12, 1919.

months and a worst-case eighteen months to build, we could see that construction on Williamson's Model A533 started sometime between the spring of 1918 and the spring of 1919. Given the architectural reengineering required to substitute twenty-four-inch for sixteen-inch balloon framing schemes, we can also assume that it took Williamson at least four to eight weeks to create construction drawings and possibly much longer. So Williamson was adapting the American System-Built Home Model B-7 into an American Renaissance Model A533 as early as December 1917, a month or a few months after leaving Milwaukee. Historian Traci Schnell adds another interesting clue. She sees evidence that Williamson was working for Richards *while* Williamson was in Kansas City, either as a side job or, more likely, as a way of laying the groundwork for a move back to Milwaukee to begin a more formal collaboration with Richards.[10]

Another home supports her theory. Starting in July 1919, a two-story Prairie-style home was built at Thirtieth Street and National Avenue in Milwaukee by the Milwaukee Realty and Construction Company—another Richards corporation—for the dentist Dr. Oscar Bellew and his wife Frances. Although the house is located just five blocks north of the Wright-Richards collaboration on the Burnham Block, the Bellews are said to have called Russell Barr Williamson their architect. Even though some secondary features were removed, the design has many similarities to the American System-Built Models N253 and N263, including proportions and layout, the roof pitch, a flowerbox with cantilevered wings, vertical exterior banding, and a pebble dash stucco finish.[11]

Indeed, in August 1918, Williamson told the Wisconsin Board of Examiners of Architects, "The preparing of several plans for Arthur L. Richards brought me to Milwaukee. And wishing to appear as the architect of certain buildings in case of publication—I found it necessary to be a Registered Architect in [Wisconsin]."[12] Williamson returned to Milwaukee in either June or July 1919 to support the building of the Bellews' house, and, significantly, the finishing details in the construction of his American Renaissance Model A533. He did not come, as we have seen, to claim the nearby American System-Built Model A203 as his own.

Therefore, while Alfred and Gladys Kibbie were moving into and finishing their unfinished Wright-designed American System-Built Home and as its builder Herman Krause and his lawyers were preparing to sue Murphy and the Kibbies, Williamson and Richards's workmen were finishing an American Renaissance House Model Number A533 *in the backyard* and using excess materials from the now defunct American

System-Built program. Because Richards was financing the project and owned the plot on which his program was being relaunched, we can assume that it was all happening on time and on budget, with no sheriffs or lawyers circling. With Wright wanting no connection with the men, there would be no argument from him. The Kibbies would have been motivated by these embarrassing developments to speed up their own cover-up.

These clues tell us that Richards believed that his vision for America was the right one, regardless of who would handle the architecture and with far less concern for original art. Richards seems to be saying that wealthier clients can have organic design, but the common man and woman should have standard windows.

This is why Williamson's name was left off the 1919 advertisement for the home on Beverly and why historians Ellias and du Fresne McArthur and Williamson's family members would find the 1922 date more fitting, despite the inaccuracy. Williamson was not licensed in Wisconsin when he was doing the architectural work to keep Richards's business going. Why search records for a home of his design before he was licensed to design it?

Moreover, Williamson saw that most architects borrow another architect's work for basic elements such as floor plans, and so for the design of his Model A533, he would too. This was a common practice that Wright himself had modeled. However, the American Renaissance home on Beverly Road reveals that Williamson was also determined to re-engineer Wright's System to be the lean and foolproof system that Richards desired. This would certainly attract more contracts from developers needing fast houses on ready plots to flip to impatient Americans at a predictable profit.

It also explains why Williamson would omit Wright from his reference list and declined to recall working on Wright's American System-Built program later in life, despite his central role in it. Wright's System was not Williamson's system. In Williamson's experience, Wright's System was slow, self-centered, and overly experimental, and it caused delays for unfortunate men like Krause and frustrated clients like Murphy and the Kibbies. Art got in the way of efficiency. Williamson's system would perform to a schedule and on a budget and do the job of housing common men and women.

In January 1921, Russell Barr Williamson wrote an article that appeared in *Concrete Magazine* featuring his design for the Eggers Bungalow, the tiny house across the street from the Elizabeth Murphy House that would sell in 1922. In it, Williamson claimed that concrete could be the basis for creative designs and layouts while offering standardization efficiencies such as interchangeable forms, common doors, and factory-made windows, though in the Eggers Bungalow and in the period he was still teetering between poured concrete and cement block, perhaps in consideration of builder preference.[13] He seems to suggest that concrete is a better, less expensive alternative to fireproofing than other methods, such as plaster containing asbestos, a substance which had not yet been reported publicly to be dangerous but still remained in short supply nearly three years after the end of World War I.

Notably, among the article's in-line drawings are three renditions of the bungalow—one featuring a flat roof, a second version with a gable roof with gutters, and a third with a hip roof, also with gutters. All built on the same footprint, just like the Wright-designed Model A201, A202, and A203. Despite moving on, Williamson had gathered up a few of the better ideas in the American System-Built program to use himself.

Most of all, we're coming closer to understanding why Frank Lloyd Wright would omit Russell Barr Williamson from his corpus, a retribution that Wright would reserve for just one man.

Versions of the Eggers Bungalow drawn by Russell Barr Williamson. In Russell Barr Williamson, "The Architecture of the Concrete House," *Concrete Magazine*, January 1921, 16.

19

The Silence

The catalog of Frank Lloyd Wright's lifelong correspondence does not contain a single entry to or from Russell Barr Williamson.[1] So either Wright culled the record, all of the records were lost in fire, or the men hardly spoke. The latter seems unlikely. So we're left with the possibility that Wright's omission of Williamson included the surgical and complete removal of evidence of the relationship from his own files. Might Wright have been the person to tear away the postscript of his sorrowful note to Ela Emerson in order to cleanse Williamson from the record?

In fact, the only mention of Williamson by Wright was not reported by Wright or an observer or saved in an archive but instead came from Williamson himself, in the same interview given in 1963 when recalling that he worked exclusively on the Imperial Hotel while in Wright's studio. Williamson said that as Wright was leaving for Japan, Wright told him, "Russell, this is the first time I have ever left (the office) with the certainty that the buildings in my office will turn out closest to what I would have done myself."[2]

Here again, we face attribution cloudiness. Who said what?

Indeed, the only reference to Williamson in the archive of Wright correspondence come from none other than Arthur L. Richards. As we have seen, Richards mentions Williamson in his 1916 plea to Wright for drawings. But beyond that, in 1945, twenty-six years after his own falling out with Wright, Richards attempted to heal old wounds.

Richards had reconnected and restarted correspondence with his former partner a few years earlier. Missed expectations, bad business, and legal wrangling were long in the past, so the older, wiser men had forgiven each other and found pleasure in sharing personal news. In fact, reconnection and reconciliation were common themes in Frank Lloyd Wright's life. After thorny separations and time to forgive, Wright reconnected with his aging mentor Louis Sullivan, his colleague Rudolph Schindler, and, in this case, with his former business partner Arthur L. Richards.[3] In the late 1930s, Richards and Wright began to exchange vacation postcards and share friendly stories of their health and places they had visited. Richards traveled to Japan, and while there, informally inspected Wright's Imperial Hotel and then wrote to Wright of its fine condition after it famously survived a massive earthquake while much of the rest of Tokyo fell. In one tender exchange, Richards announced his retirement from the drudgery of construction work and told Wright, "Yours is the work of an artist (which you are), and is always interesting."[4] The men shared clippings of articles about architecture, favorite books to read (they exchanged and discussed Clarence Darrow's biography), and reflections on the people with whom they remembered working.

Richards took the opportunity to make another plea, again in a gentle hand, for reconciliation between Wright and Williamson. By then, Williamson had fallen on hard times. Business had dried up and foreclosure had forced him out of his Prairie-style family home in Whitefish Bay, Wisconsin. Richards had come to Williamson's rescue with affordable housing—an apartment in a hotel in downtown Milwaukee for Russell, Nola Mae, and the kids—and hoped that Wright would step in with a kind word of support for his assistant from long ago.[5]

In a short note to Wright on April 20, 1945, Richards wrote, "I am also enclosing some of our circulars showing what we have been doing, a new *American* home, by *Russell*. I really think if you see it you will be O.K. with it."[6]

Wright apparently did not respond.

20

The Submission

Frank Lloyd Wright had been prescient when grumbling about speculation just before tiptoeing into it cautiously with his System.

In his 1914 article "In the Cause of Architecture," Wright observed, "The average American man or woman who wants to build a house wants something different . . . and most of them want it in a hurry." But he also saw that this resulted in poor architecture. He added that the work of architects on behalf of developers "has been showing weaknesses instead of the character it might have shown some years hence, were it more enlightened and discreet, more sincere and modest, prepared to wait, to wait to prepare."[1]

To wait to prepare, from Wright's perspective, was to make room for creativity. Artists enjoying the favor of a patient patron would enjoy the room to experiment and refine and then to decide when their art was ready. However, given that most Americans did not or would not have the time or resources to carve out such room, architects taking their commissions indiscriminately would have to compromise design for speed.

It is worth repeating an earlier quotation from the same article while reflecting on its timing and symbolism: "I dread seeing the types I have worked with so long and patiently, drifting toward speculative builders."

At the time that Wright's article was hitting the presses, Russell Williamson was working in Wright's studio, predominantly on Arthur Richards's projects, which included speculations and speculators as customers. Richards would soon sell plans to Elizabeth Murphy, who would eventually flip her investment to Alfred and Gladys Kibbie.

The Kibbies wanted a house. What they got, instead and far too late, was precious art. Living in that art and lacking a connection to its origins would become at best an inconvenience and at worst an embarrassment crossing generations.

Still, Wright had predicted their plight. So he preemptively called for action in his 1914 article compelling his architectural peers, critics, and apprentices—especially his apprentices—to empathize with people like the Kibbies and consider a better way to meet their needs.

The American System-Built experience confirmed what Wright had suspected: that distance and detachment from the people who would occupy his homes risked his art. Wright hoped the System would emphasize affordable beauty, but Richards's interpretation instead created distance and therefore systematized anonymity by selling houses anywhere, and everywhere, to anyone and as fast as they might be assembled.

Wright, lacking a direct connection to the Kibbies, could not set their expectations, inform or appeal to their taste or timing, or make an artisan's case for patronage, patience, or, most important, reverence. He was not assuming that the Kibbies were not capable of such things. That was something he could not know. Instead, Wright was prevented—by his own System—from receiving them as their architect.

After all, what would prevent owners like the Kibbies from covering up one of Wright's masterpieces? As we know, nothing did. Lacking a relationship with the artist, they had no motive to advocate for the art in their architecture—no preservation incentive or reason to conserve—and therefore, Wright's work would inevitably be lost.

On the other hand, Williamson, with his direct connection to the Kibbies, saw their plight only in a utilitarian light and doubled down on a truly American system: a machine made for speed that Wright knew would suffer compromise and, inevitably, experiential mediocrity and artistic anonymity. Williamson had determined that the Kibbies didn't need what Wright was offering because, from his perspective, the Kibbies were not the customers—Richards was. To Wright, this was a deep-cutting insult both to the homeowners and to the artist who had designed their home.

Like Wright before him, Williamson would start his independent career by selecting and adapting some of the ideas of a mentor while straddling the line between appropriation and original work. On large homes for wealthy clients, Williamson's early works are still often confused with Wright's, especially from the street.

Imitation, in and of itself, was not the crucial factor for Wright in assessing Williamson and would not fuel Wright's retribution. In "In the Cause of Architecture," Wright said:

> One may submit to the flattery of imitation or to caricature personally; everyone who marches or strays from beaten paths must submit to one or both, but never will one submit tamely to caricature of that which one loves.[2]

From Wright's perspective, imitation was just another consideration in the work of design—an application of experience within artistic expression. It might be done well, it would be worse if done poorly, but it would be done. Wright's main concern was that an architect should demonstrate that he or she could see and understand the problem, conceive of or embrace a solution, and ensure that the solution be conspicuous. A decent copy should at least carry forward (and not lose sight of) the purposeful solutions contained in its source design. In this case, Williamson had not proven to Wright that he understood the vital ingredients in Wright's System. Wright mourned that for modest homes for modest folks, Williamson, alongside Richards, had hacked up his elegant architectural System, hamstrung the artistry, and cut essential organic elements—like sunlight and garden views—into what he saw as "ungainly caricatures," giving the remaining benefits to sales representatives for the sake of sales.

Williamson had revealed himself to Wright as naive and gullible to the speculator, as Wright had predicted an apprentice might. Not a thief or too ambitious, just a callow and impressionable lackey. The middle-aged Wright sized up the young man and determined that he would not become a competitor, a conspirator, or an archenemy in the work of organic design.

Indeed, Wright was himself evolving out of the Prairie style into Mayan and deeper Asian influences, energized by the experience of travel and culture.[3] The Wright biographer Henry-Russell Hitchcock reflected about the time that "neither [Wright's] genius nor his personality fitted any longer in the middle-class frame, perhaps in any case growing more hidebound, of the suburban Middle West. Frank Lloyd Wright, no longer of Oak Park, but of resurgent Taliesin, was ready to serve the world."[4]

Discovery was offering Wright an opportunity to reinvent himself at the time when he most needed it.

Williamson would not follow because he could not follow. He was landlocked. According to his wife Nola Mae, Russell had been kept from traveling to Japan with Wright for fear of a missed paycheck, thereby missing the opportunity to see and experience other cultures that would inform fresh interpretations.[5] And because they could not and would not work together, Wright could not teach him.

Williamson simply became the man unworthy of mention.

Central to this omission: the defining characteristics of the men. Wright found footing in and would leave a global legacy of inspired art, but he was a messy businessman. Williamson started his career alongside the savvy local tycoon Richards, whose main concern was return on investment, so Williamson's design work needed to be only adequate to ensure a profitable sale.

This is not to say that Williamson was ineffective. Quite the contrary. He would leave a voluminous mark on Wisconsin, influencing midwestern and suburban aesthetics and lifestyles to this day. Almost 120 attractive homes shelter contented Wisconsin families from Racine to Oconomowoc to Sheboygan, including handsome bungalows and Milwaukee flats and the largest Mediterranean Revival mansion on Whitefish Bay's posh Lake Drive. Williamson's signature Eagles Club in Milwaukee remains a popular concert hall, and stars still twinkle from the ceiling of the elegant Avalon Atmospheric Theater in the city's Bay View neighborhood.[6]

Ironically, Williamson would enjoy a comparatively robust local business designing homes for suburban developers in the decade that followed the Murphy fiasco, while Wright's business remained sluggish and far-flung. Within ten years of moving to the Milwaukee area, Williamson was the named architect on at least fifty-four projects: fifty-two single-family homes and duplexes in suburbs such as Shorewood, Whitefish Bay, and Wauwatosa, along with the aforementioned Eagles Club and the Avalon Theater. Wright would work on only fourteen projects in the same period, though usually of a larger scale and all over the map.

Williamson's willingness to work for speculators played in his favor for a time, but in a tragic twist, it was a speculation that nearly destroyed his blossoming career. On February 8, 1929, Williamson announced that construction would begin on a new eight-story "skyscraper" featuring double-deck parking and luxury bungalow apartments with lake and river views, to be located at the corner of Oakland and Glendale Avenues, three blocks south of his own home and one mile north of the Elizabeth Murphy House.[7] It would tower over the neighborhood that he had shaped and would stand as his signature piece—the tallest, grandest building on the north shore. Though little is written about it (his children did not even know about it), the project and concept seemed to have been his baby; his design, his management, seeded with his own money, and so therefore, his speculation. If Richards was involved as an investor or partner, he had elected to take a silent backseat to Williamson's potent local brand. But Williamson revealed the plan to the press on the same day that the Federal Reserve warned that an "excessive amount of the country's credit [is] absorbed in speculative loans," and stocks began to tumble.[8] Within months the market crashed, Williamson's project was canceled, and he filed for bankruptcy. While the Great Depression would call off architectural contracts everywhere, Williamson wouldn't see regular work again for almost two decades, holding the household together on piecework remodeling and millwork plans. A gas station was built on the corner instead. Finally, Williamson's career restarted in the 1950s with projects to design post–World War II apartment buildings, banks, ranch-style homes, and one-off commissions in a variety of styles, sprinkled mostly in Wisconsin cities and towns. In his 1963 interview with the *Milwaukee Sentinel*'s David Link, Williamson said he had learned that direct client engagement was important to a lasting and loved design—a conclusion he announced, ironically, in the last years of a nearly fifty-year career.

Today, Russell Barr Williamson's architectural contribution remains frustratingly enigmatic to historians trying to find and characterize his work and life. Apart from attributed extant buildings, public records, and a few local stories, there are too few continuous stylistic threads, too many gaps, and too many dead ends. A final project inventory seems impossible. This is why Williamson's son and granddaughter were unable to declare a complete list, why Juanita Ellias chose Williamson as the subject of her thesis, and why sleuths like Richard Johnson drove around century-old neighborhoods hoping to uncover clues. A true and total Williamson résumé is bedeviled by the fact that he did not claim work that he should have claimed, he may have claimed work not his, he chose not to save records, and the records that may have been saved by his lifelong friend Arthur L. Richards were lost too.

Williamson's 1918 omission of Wright and Wright's omission of him sealed that fate.

After the Elizabeth Murphy project fiasco and the end of the American System-Built program, Wright turned his attention back to one large commission after another and works for the wealthy to buy time to return to the challenge of modest home design when he had better footing. His immensely successful Usonian homes were to come.

Wright would come to view the American System-Built episode through the lens of design; the challenge was still to bring beauty in small and affordable packages. How could he democratize the business of architecture while protecting the artistic value in the work? To do that, he would need to distinguish democracy from capitalism.

As it is designed to do, capitalism had co-opted a good system for its own benefit while taking victims. Wright's System began as a method of optimistic egalitarian architecture intended to empower the creative architect to reform America and help spread the American dream, but American capitalism took a cruel bite out of it and spit it back in an unworkable form, unrecognizable and unpalatable to the idealist.

For Wright, affordability was a path to an enlightened populace. The American system—Richards's capitalistic system—instead saw profit margin and took it, at the expense of enlightenment. The Kibbies' jarring response to their troublesome home may have haunted Wright but was of no consequence to Richards. That investors like Murphy and suppliers and builders like Krause had lost money on the project was the luck of the draw as far as Richards was concerned. Markets are ruthless.

Historians have said that an American System-Built Home might have cost 20 percent less to buy than other homes at the time.[9] Even today, 20 percent would be a rich return on investment for someone with a plot of land to flip and a contractor willing to take a fixed-price contract to build a house on it. For Wright, this was cynical math, and it still worried him in 1957 when he wrote:

> The urban realtor now looms as future America's most obstinate enemy. . . . Quantity is entrenched by him to put an end to quality. . . . The insolence of authority is endeavoring to substitute money for ideas.[10]

Although he would eventually forgive Richards the man, Richards the "urban realtor" had created a system to solicit investors and friends to exploit Wright's System, relegating American cities to mediocrity and Americans to uninspired and dreary lives. To organize mass production and mass sale, Richards needed a planner, not an artist. Russell Williamson didn't know it in 1917, but he was being swallowed by Richards's American system—a cruel machine that he was helping to assemble. Wright could not extract him from its jaws.

Wright appears to have learned many lessons from the episode:

- Machines could be enlisted to make better buildings; but the machine of capitalism, which was designed to put money first, would never produce a piece of lasting original art. Wright would continue to experiment with materials, tools, and methods, but he stayed out of markets.
- The artist must never lose control over anything used in the creation of the art. Wright would famously retake control over as many of the

details of a project as possible: visiting sites, selecting plots, designing furniture, and creating his own color palettes.

- To secure a legacy as a great artist, an artist must find clients whose appreciation for and love of the work ensures the care and feeding of it no matter how big or expensive or time-consuming the effort to care for it is. True attribution depends on experience, whereas anonymity suffers experience and the lack of experience suffers anonymity, so clients could not be strangers. Wright would need to know them.

In this context, we can see how and why Wright omitted the System and, tellingly, erased the word *American* from his design vocabulary.

Another letter in the Avery collection explains.

In 1955, thirty-seven years after the end of the American System-Built program, a publicist named Betty Kassler wrote to Wright with a request. She had been asked by a French publisher to collect materials for a book about American houses and was proposing three of Wright's designs as examples to feature. She hoped to discuss the "structural geometry" and needed permission to contact photographers. It was a simple and friendly request.

Wright replied:

> Dear Betty: What a nuisance you publicists are. We have no wish to be classified with "American houses"—the bastards.
>
> Love to you both,
> Frank Lloyd Wright[11]

Wright omitted everything about the American System-Built Homes program. He never mentioned the homes. He severed relations with its contributors and covered his tracks. And he blamed America for corrupting the art of designing homes for people of modest means.

He would wait for the day when he could purify and elevate that complex work to its rightful place by doing it as it should be done.

21

The Legacy

We moved into the Elizabeth Murphy House on December 23, 2016, and within a week had heard from the organizers at Wright in Wisconsin—the local chapter of Wrightophiles—with a request that the home be included on the upcoming "Wright and Like" tour scheduled for June 2017. The annual tour features select homes by Wright, his apprentices, and architects he influenced. The tour organizers would supply docents, safety, publicity, crowd control; everything *except* the work to make the house ready. Our house needed years of work that the deadline made happen in six months. We pulled carpets, scraped up old linoleum and chiseled off faux bricks glued to a kitchen wall in the 1970s, pulled down the blinds, filled nail holes, removed window air conditioners, and replaced the windows they had annexed. We patched and painted every wall and ceiling and much of the weathered exterior. We removed every inch of rusted and decrepit galvanized supply plumbing and replaced it with copper. We refinished floors to period stains and colors. And, as you know from chapter 8, we renovated the bathroom.

With just a month before the tour, I came home from work and panicked: We could *not* open the house to a crowd of visitors, some who would be serious Wrightophiles, until we fixed the garage or at least its ugliest elements.

Elizabeth Murphy must have thought cars would not be necessary for citizens of Shorewood; the house she built had no garage or carport and no place to add one (despite a selection of optional carriage houses included in the American System-Built Homes catalog). In 1917, trolleys ran north, south, and west from East Milwaukee. Alfred Kibbie would ride one from the Shorewood Station to the Trostel Company for decades, until he worked up the ranks to become its vice president. By then, he and Gladys had moved to another house in Shorewood that had a garage, and both girls were grown up, married, and starting families nearby.

In 1917, cars were not omnipresent except among the wealthy. Everyone seemed to expect that the common man and woman would always prefer or at least be relegated to public transportation.

By the 1970s the world had changed; the consumption economy was in full swing, and the then owners of the Elizabeth Murphy House needed to park their car. Out of necessity, they excavated part of the front yard and the space under the sleeping porch to create a driveway and a garage. Thankfully, they did it without disturbing anything in the house above, and today their work can be credited with stabilizing the foundation under the porch where the footings were shallowest and therefore beginning to shift.

However, in a clumsy attempt to tie the garage to the house, a ground-level eyebrow roof was added to the facade just above the garage door and below the sleeping porch windows, held up by two fat concrete block columns covered in stucco. Over the years the columns had shifted and the brow sagged, like a lazy eye. Indeed, cracks, odd angles, and layers of caulk caused home inspectors for other prospective buyers to conclude that the foundation was compromised. In fact, the facade was the only thing moving. It was as if the house was rejecting a skin transplant. We could see from our own inspection that the columns were merely cosmetic.

Not wanting tourgoers to assume the worst, I was determined to clean it up. At a minimum I would grind out and patch the ugliest cracks. As layers came off and the extent of the trouble and the subsequent effort to mask the mess became clear, I decided instead to tear it all off. As sledgehammer hit concrete block, you could hear the home breathe a sigh of relief. Angela returned from errands to a bit of a surprise. The street-level garage facade was now a large pile of debris in the driveway.

For the rest of the weekend, we mixed mortar, parged walls, and cut and painted matching trim. Within days, the Elizabeth Murphy House stood tall and straight and ready for tourgoers, the cracks and sags gone, the garage door deemphasized and the glorious house above reemphasized, straight and true.

In the midst of our demolition, a car slowly pulled up, and a gentleman emerged to introduce himself as the son of Teddy Kibbie. He could see that we were busy, so we shared only a few stories. He told us that Teddy had been courted by her high school sweetheart (his father) on our front (side) steps. He said that his grandfather Alfred felt strongly about affordability and didn't think it was right to profit from a modest, sturdy, but beautiful home designed for the working class. He and Gladys had paid about $5,000 in 1918, and then they sold the house in 1942 to the next owners for about $5,000.

It should be said, however, that the Kibbies would find utility in pedigree to create demand for the home when it came time to sell. Their advertisement in the May 2, 1941, *Milwaukee Sentinel* read, "We offer you a genuine Frank Lloyd Wright home in one of the choicest parts of Shorewood."[1]

We agreed to reconvene on another day, when Teddy Kibbie's son had more time to see the home where his mom had grown up.

Teddy's son's short stories helped us find the final clues in our historical mystery. They were in the powers of affordability and the personal relationship to democratize the art.

In 1936, Herbert Jacobs, a journalist, met and challenged Frank Lloyd Wright to design a home for him and his wife Katherine that could be built for $5,000, and Wright answered with the masterpiece now called Usonia One in Madison, Wisconsin, named a UNESCO World Heritage Site in 2019.[2] Jacobs's challenge would kick off Wright's second program to design breathtaking homes for people of modest means. The $5,000 target provided little room for error, and there were overruns and delays on the Jacobs project. Famously, Wright would address those troubles quickly by taking some of the rejected bricks from the job site of the massive SC Johnson project, which was also under way at the time, to use them on the Jacobs home. It was a solution that neither Krause nor Wright could offer to the Kibbies via Elizabeth Murphy and Arthur Richards.

There is no small irony in the fact that the Elizabeth Murphy House sold for the same $5,000 price in 1918 and 1942, both before *and after* Usonia One was built for about $5,000 in 1937.[3] In fact, Jacobs later said that when he asked Wright to build a $5,000 home, Wright told him that he had been waiting decades for someone to ask just that question.[4] Of course, the Kibbies *had* asked exactly that question, but they had directed their inquiry to Elizabeth Murphy, and she worked with Arthur Richards to give them an answer, so Wright had never heard it from them.

In Usonia One, we learn *how* Wright would correct the flaws he had uncovered in the American System-Built program and how he invented a small-scale populist architecture that still inspires today.

He began by proposing something bigger than an American brand, system, machine, or market and offered instead a new democratic architecture—a process rooted in the spirit and potential of the nation's land and all its people. The word *Usonia* would loosely abbreviate to the "United States of America," conjuring utopian images of natural spaces and places; the diversity of the landscape, its trees, water, and rocks; and its languages and cultures. He unified those elements into a singular aesthetic ethos that evolved and grew until his death while creating a new standard for all American neighborhoods and cities and, most important, elevating the expectations of aspirational and discerning working men and women. If America was to be a beacon, then its dreamers should be able to live in dignity, comfort, and beauty and be trusted to care for original art.

With Usonia One, Wright reshuffled his client approach, in effect promoting owners from recipients of a home to its stewards. Collaboration was not to be the exclusive purview of the wealthy; instead, the frugal, modest, practical Jacobses would work alongside Wright to get the space and the life that they desired. The planned experience of planning was so brilliant and inspired that the Jacobses would try a second time, designing Usonia Two with Wright in 1943. The work was said to be not always pleasant, but the outcomes were spectacular.

Wright's response was inspired and strategic, albeit hard to see—hidden in plain sight, like the Elizabeth Murphy House itself—because it took decades to play out and to reveal itself.

Wright removed the middleman and middlewoman. He asked for and received patience. He defanged the profit motive by sidestepping the speculator to redirect finite dollars to the most important work of listening, empathetic design, consensus building, and high-quality products. He went right to the people, heard their wants and needs, shared his ideas, set clear expectations, and then unleashed limitless creativity to meet the affordability challenge while creating an unforgettable lifelong experience in the making of and the living in a modest single-family home. Participation, he found, engendered not just ownership but also stewardship. Here we can see that easy and fast are easily and quickly forgotten and therefore disposable, but hard things—things that take time—like fresh plans and novel concepts forged in conversation, have the potential to result in something artful, loved, and lasting.

It was everything Wright could neither do with nor expect from the Kibbies.

Libraries of books have been written about Usonian homes, and we will not elaborate on that established history here. That is for the experts. It is sufficient to summarize. By studying the place where the people would live, Wright could see how to create a space that would fit both the land and their lives. By sourcing local and common materials, Wright shrank and stabilized the supply chain. By integrating systems like heat into floors, furniture into walls, and cars into ports, he removed parts and pieces, simplifying both the building and the living experience. By creating a small but open space with walls of light, views in key directions, organic themes and motifs, paths for people to discover and the sun to travel, pathways in which to compress and release, social and intimate areas, two bedrooms and a six-by-six-foot bathroom, and only a few places to keep important things, Wright helped the Jacobses to live deliberately, as was their wish.

And as he has done for us.

But most important, by directly engaging with the clever albeit common folk who would occupy his homes, he would discover the reverence—the patronage offered by and the patience contained within the working American man and woman—that helped Wright learn to trust the people to care for his art and to ensure his monumental place in history.

22

The Man with the Hat

Late in September 2016, Angela and I submitted our offer to purchase Pat Wisialowski's Frank Lloyd Wright–designed home, along with a commitment letter, summarized below:

> Dear Mrs. Wisialowski,
>
> We came to Shorewood twenty-one years ago to raise our kids among lovely neighbors and homes like yours. We lovingly upgraded our own home and gardens, I built businesses nearby and Angela became the Art Teacher at Atwater School, where she teaches Shorewood children about local art and architecture, among other things. One of her class projects is to recreate Shorewood facades in clay after hiking neighborhoods, talking about history and engineering, and making 2D pencil sketches. Hundreds of colorful miniatures of familiar homes rest on Shorewoodian fireplace mantels alongside student-signed architectural renderings as provenance.
>
> With our adult daughters now in college, we are entering a new chapter: we plan to stay in Shorewood, where we hope to give back. We think your home is an important key.
>
> Like you, we plan to be attentive and careful stewards and archivists while we live at 2106 East Newton. We will protect its glory, celebrate its importance, and secure its future. We plan to study every detail of Wright's plans and workmanship and make sure that they remain intact and fresh. We will invest in and care for the home and yard as an important artistic and civic statement.

> To that end, Angela is already supplementing her curriculum to teach students about Wright's vision, genius and aesthetic through her own experience of living in it. We have read every word written about the home since it was re-discovered and will continue to engage the experts to try to uncover new clues and details about its place in our neighborhood. The home will remain a well-cared-for showpiece, although it will not be trampled by tourists. It will stay a private, quiet neighborhood gem, while also, importantly, creating a direct, tangible teaching moment for local kids.

Pat kindly accepted our offer, and eleven months later, on a blustery fall day, the first fifty fourth graders from Atwater School walked four blocks with teacher and parent chaperones to tour our tiny home, stopping along the way to study and catalog such architectural details as columns, chimneys, and cornices on neighboring homes, many designed by Frank Lloyd Wright's former assistant, Russell Barr Williamson.

At the Elizabeth Murphy House, they experienced compression before release, twice. They clustered in and talked about the sparkly ceiling, the Place of Greeting, and the fireplace at the heart of the home, and when Mrs. Hayes asked what image from nature they saw in the art glass, one said a rose, another said a tulip, and a third said a tree. A fourth kid raised his hand and said, "I don't see nature, but I do see a man with a hat." It was as if Mr. Wright was finally acknowledging the place with a personal visit, making himself known to all standing in it. Such is the risk and the reward of abstraction.

A few days after their tour of the house, Mrs. Hayes led a field trip to Madison, where they explored the Frank Lloyd Wright floor of the Madison Children's Museum. There, the kids used blocks to build cantilevers and catenary arches and played games in the geometric spaces that model Wright's own studio in order to experience biomimicry firsthand. Some dressed as Frank, donning his coat, his porkpie hat, and his cane.

After their field trip the kids returned to the classroom to draw two-dimensional sketches of an imaginary home; their own creative interpretation informed by their research and experience. Then they

Fourth graders in Mrs. Hayes's art class arriving at the Frank Lloyd Wright–designed Elizabeth Murphy House to study local architecture, October 9, 2019. Photo by Nicholas Hayes.

molded their ideas into clay using a variety of textures and modeling techniques such as slabs, spheres, and coils. The clay pieces were fired and then glazed and then fired again to reveal personal color palettes. Many of the pieces were hung a few months later at the Shorewood Public Library as part of the annual School District Art Show to be seen and admired by hundreds of neighbors.

Just as Wright had planned every inch of your virtual tour of our home many chapters back, Mrs. Hayes, its new steward, planned every minute of the experience shared by her fourth-grade students. Frank Lloyd Wright was planning so as to encourage authentic living. Mrs. Hayes plans so as to encourage authentic *learning*. These are not meaningfully different concepts.

Speaking for myself, I fell into stewardship with vague and unremarkable expectations. My limited understanding of fine architecture was naive and even skeptical. I had toured and admired the Wright-designed

Annunciation Greek Orthodox Church, Taliesin East, the Guggenheim Museum, and the Dana House, and they were all amazing. But how could a space make daily life better? Isn't authenticity a product of people and not place?

Wright knew better.

Place—and more specifically, *space*—matters, because it has the capacity to move people closer to each other, or to new ideas, or to new and better ways of living. Space can either inhibit a social experience or, done well, enable meaningful social engagement and deeper relationship. We witness this happening every time friends, family, and public-school fourth graders visit, and especially when a person stands for the first time in the Place of Greeting and ponders what is happening then and there. We are awestruck that his impact is being felt over a century later.

Elizabeth Murphy could not have known that her name would become the name of a historic home hiding secrets for a century. She could not have predicted that her terribly tardy project would become the scene of a mysterious drama that would alter relationships and biographies, reshape Wright's life and legacy, and influence contemporary American suburban living. Nor could she have known that her failed investment in a narrow parcel of land in Shorewood, Wisconsin, would be returning priceless, grand benefits today. Every fall fourth graders visit to see the "man with the hat" in the art glass windows and experience his art. Then, if they choose, they may gather up a few of his better ideas to carry forward into their own.

Epilogue

In January 2020, the owners-stewards of five American System-Built Homes gathered at the Guy C. Smith House on Chicago's South Side for a tour, a tasty lunch, and the opportunity to trade stories. We share a special kinship built on similar but uncommon experiences. Everyone has a story of a stranger knocking on the door expecting to be given an on-the-spot tour. Many of us have watched groups of astonished, giggling visitors cram into our bathrooms to experience the tiny spaces during organized tours. Every home has its quirks: one was a "model" home in their neighborhood and was featured in 1917 advertisements, another was designed to have a door on the side but was spun 90 degrees by the builder to seem more conventional. Many homes have details that seem to be off-plan, and most, but not all, were built speculatively. Most of us have studied the drawings at the Avery Museum, entertained a visit from Mike Lilek, read Shirley du Fresne McArthur's book, gone to Frank Lloyd Wright Building Conservancy conferences, traced the history of homeownership, and been subjected to questions about the legitimacy of our homes as truly Wrightian. The question of legitimacy can be disheartening to hear as an invested and loving caretaker, but it is a fair question. With spotty records and Wright's disavowal, what are the thresholds of pedigree? If pressed, Wright might not have willingly claimed any of our homes, and yet they are his inspiration and genius. If Picasso had sketched on the back sleeve of a dime store novel and it was later unearthed at a thrift shop, the art would still be Picasso's.

Meanwhile, the search for more American System-Built Homes is not over and is gaining urgency as the homes enter their second century. A private Facebook group for fans of Frank Lloyd Wright often features a new drive-by image of a modest and sometimes decrepit or grossly modified Prairie-style bungalow or two-family dwelling with the question, "Is this a long lost ASBH?" I've taken to walking the same streets that Richard Johnson drove in the hopes of uncovering another hidden gem; anything window-clad with long overhangs and a big chimney deserves further scrutiny.

We hope that every American System-Built Home can one day be accounted for and that the information we have presented here will help in that detective work. Researchers have much to work with, including Wright's determination to safeguard his designs and the dates whereby the court agreed and ruled that all the American System-Built Homes and the System of Construction to make them were his inventions and exclusive property. The opening of the Frank Lloyd Wright Foundation Archives at the Avery Museum provides many new windows to shine light on Wright's dark years. However, we may never see Arthur Richards's or Russell Barr Williamson's records, so there is still a gray area in knowing how many of Wright's ideas remained in the homes credited to Williamson and sold by Richards in the years 1919 to 1928. The research will need to be both spacious and surgical in how it considers evolution and evidence.

Most important, we wish for the story of the Elizabeth Murphy House to inspire new and deeper studies of Wright's early creative processes; how his leadership and communication styles and his approach to engineering and client engagement evolved and how these forgotten homes—and their countless offspring, the places that shelter the families all around us—have shaped our American dreams.

Acknowledgments

Thanks to the Frank Lloyd Wright Building Conservancy, the Frank Lloyd Wright Foundation, the Avery Architectural and Fine Arts Library at Columbia University, the First Unitarian Society of Milwaukee, the Getty Research Institute, the Milwaukee County Historical Society, the Shorewood Historical Society, the Wisconsin Historical Society, the Madison Children's Museum, Jeff Aiken, Suzanne Bost, Michael Desmond, Cheryl DeWelt, Don Ellingsen, Mary Ellingsen, Barbara Gordon, Charles Guadagnino, Peter Halper, Elizabeth Jane Hayes, Katherine Rose Hayes, John Edward Hayes, Emira Nako Hayes, Philia Geotes Hayes, John Gilmore Hayes, Mark Hertzberg, Michael Horne, Richard Johnson, Kathy Kean, Michael Lilek, Patricia Lilek, Jason Loper, Linda McQuillen, Debra and David Nemeth, Joe Picciolo, Michael Pipher, Mathieu Pomerleau, Katherine Prater, Linda Presto, Steve Schaffer, Traci Schnell, Michael Schreiber, Marsha Shyer, Margaret Smithglass, Aaron Stark, Sara Stathas, Margo Stipe, Dr. William Allin Storrer, Karen von Huene, John Waters, Stuart Wick, Mike Wilk, Katie Bailey Wilk, Patricia Wisialowski, and Robert and Patricia Wozniak.

Special thanks to my dad, the journalist Paul Gordon Hayes, for reading and editing every draft of this story and for insisting on solid research and basic English.

And in fond memory of Dorothy (Stock) Hoffman (1924–2020).

Chronology, 1914–19

In Milwaukee	*Month/Year*	*In Wright's Universe*
	June 1914	Russell Barr Williamson joins Wright's Chicago office
	August 1914	Taliesin fire kills Wright's mistress, Mamah Borthwick, and others there and destroys many Wright records
Burnham Block American System-Built Home (ASBH) construction started on tract of land purchased by Wright colleague Arthur L. Richards	October 1915	Three Wright designs part of Burnham Block
	May 1916	Some ASBH drawings reviewed and approved, including Model A203 (May 9) Russell Williamson and Nola Mae Hawthorne married (May 20)
Burnham Block ASBH construction completed	July 1916	
Construction begins on Bogk House, a Wright-designed Prairie-style home (not ASBH) promoted by Richards, with Williamson as supervisor	August 1916	

In Milwaukee	*Month/Year*	*In Wright's Universe*
	September 1916	Wright gives speech in Chicago touting the American System-Built Homes
Construction begins on Munkwitz Apartments, an ASBH project at Twenty-seventh Street and Highland Avenue in Milwaukee, with Williamson as supervisor	October 1916	
	November 1916	With Burnham Block complete, Wright and Richards begin to work under sales/manufacturing agreement to sell ASBHs in the United States, Canada, and Europe
	December 1916	Wright leaves for Japan to prepare for Imperial Hotel construction, leaving Williamson in charge of Milwaukee projects (and others in charge of ongoing projects in other cities)
Bogk House finished *Milwauke Journal* features Munkwitz Apartments (January 21)	January 1917	Richards sends handwritten note to Wright begging for more drawing time and promising to send partial due payments (January 1)
	February 1917	Richards sends typewritten update letter to Wright restating urgent need for drawings, reporting progress, and suggesting one project under way (February 6)

In Milwaukee	*Month/Year*	*In Wright's Universe*
Investor Elizabeth Murphy and carpenter-contractor Herman Krause agree to build Wright-designed Model A203 ASBH home at 440 Newton Avenue in Shorewood (March 31)	March 1917	
Construction begins on Elizabeth Murphy House (April 20)	April 1917	Wright returns from Japan
The Munkwitz Apartments completed		
Assignment of lien on 440 Newton from Richards to Landeck Lumber puts Murphy project at risk (June 4)	June 1917	No commissions paid to Wright for ASBH sales—per Wright letter
		Richards attempts to sell shares of stock
	July 1917	No commissions paid to Wright for ASBH sales—per Wright letter
	August 1917	Wright sends letter to Richards terminating agreements and cancels program (August 10)
		Wright sues Richards for due commissions and legally terminates their contract (August 11)
	September 1917	Injunction filed to prevent Richards from using plans and specifications except for projects under way (September 1)
	November 1917	Williamson quits or is let go and takes a railroad job in Kansas City
	February 1918	Lawsuit results in judgment for Wright, who is paid $1,581.05 in commissions (February 25)

In Milwaukee	*Month/Year*	*In Wright's Universe*
Krause walks off Murphy's job site (October 15) and doesn't return, leaving much of interior work unfinished	October 1918	
	November 1918	Wright returns to Japan to supervise start of Imperial Hotel construction
Krause files a lien on the property to collect monies due for labor and materials supplied	April 1919	
	May 1919	Richards and Williamson agree that Williamson should return to Milwaukee to start new business and practice
	June 1919	Construction under way on Williamson-designed American Renaissance Inc. Model A533, a model bearing many similarities to Wright-designed ASBH Model B-7, at Murray Avenue and Beverly Road in Shorewood
Murphy deems house "ready for sale"	July 1919	Construction begins on Bellew House at Thirtieth and National in Milwaukee
Murphy completes land contract for sale of property at 440 Newton Avenue to Alfred and Gladys Kibbie, who take possession	August 1919	Williamson writes letter to Board of Examiners from Richards's office requesting Wisconsin state architect's license (August 4)
Krause lawsuit filed against Murphy and Kibbies (September 17)	September 1919	
	October 1919	American Renaissance Inc. Model A533 available for inspection (October 12)
	November 1919	Williamson receives his Wisconsin architect's license

Notes

Chapter 1. The Announcement

1. Mark Hoffman, "Wisconsin Couple Discovers Home Was Designed by Frank Lloyd Wright," Associated Press, 2015.

2. Bobby Tanzillo, "Shorewood House Identified as a Rare Frank Lloyd Wright Design," *On Milwaukee*, June 5, 2015, https://onmilwaukee.com/buzz/articles/franklloydwrightshorewoodhome.html.

3. Michael Horne, "Shorewood's 'New' Frank Lloyd Wright Home," *Urban Milwaukee*, July 10, 2015, https://urbanmilwaukee.com/2015/06/10/house-confidential-shorewoods-new-frank-lloyd-wright-home/.

Chapter 3. Wright's America

1. Frank Lloyd Wright, *The Sovereignty of the Individual* (Ausgeführte Bauten und Entwürfe, 1910).

2. Frank Lloyd Wright, "In the Cause of Architecture," *Architectural Record* 35, no. 5 (May 1914), 409.

3. Hugh Morrison, *Louis Sullivan: Prophet of Modern Architecture* (W. W. Norton, 1935), 34.

4. Frank Lloyd Wright, "The American System of House Building," *Western Architect* 24 (September 1916), 122.

5. Frank Lloyd Wright, *An Autobiography* (Duell, Sloan and Pearce, 1943), 168.

6. Frank Lloyd Wright, "The Mike Wallace Interview," 1957, https://www.youtube.com/watch?v=DeKzIZAKG3E.

7. Fred A. Bernstein, "The Last Original Frank Lloyd Wright Owners," *Wall Street Journal Magazine*, February 2017.

8. Wright, "The American System of House Building," 121.

Chapter 4. The Americans

1. Michael Lilek reproduced a classified advertisement from the December 15, 1918, issue of the *Milwaukee Journal* on page 11 of his *2106 East Newton Avenue, Shorewood, Wisconsin: An American System-Built House Model A203* (self-published, 2015), https://elizabethmurphyhouse.files.wordpress.com/2017/11/2106_newton_research_20150603.pdf. Underscores in the classified ad indicate illegible characters. Although not visible, the asking price was probably $5,500. Streets and houses in Shorewood were subsequently renumbered, so 400 Newton became 2106 East Newton Avenue the next year.

2. *Copperdome, the Student Yearbook of Shorewood High School*, 1941, Shorewood Historical Society Archive, Shorewood, Wisconsin.

3. *Copperdome*, 1938, 1941.

4. On Parent Teacher Association, see "Social," *Suburban Herald*, April 6, 1933, 4; on Shorewood Women's Club, see "News of the Week," *Shorewood Herald*, May 16, 1940, 2; on Shorewood Welfare Association play to "aid the needy," see "Rehearsals for Charity Play Begin Saturday," *Shorewood Herald*, November 2, 1933, 1; all in Shorewood Historical Society Archive.

5. Dorothy Hoffmann, conversations with the author, June 2017.

6. Hoffmann conversations with the author, June 2017.

Chapter 5. The Tour

1. In the ancient Japanese Shinto religious tradition, a Torii gate is the entrance to a shrine.

2. "Specifications of Materials and Labor Required for the American Model ____ in Accordance with Drawings Prepared by Frank Lloyd Wright, Architect," FLWFA Specs Box 2, 1112–1903, Frank Lloyd Wright Foundation Archives, Museum of Modern Art, Avery Architectural and Fine Arts Library, Columbia University, New York.

3. Wright, *An Autobiography*, 198.

Chapter 6. The System

1. Shirley du Fresne McArthur, *Frank Lloyd Wright: American System-Built Homes in Milwaukee* (North Point Historical Society, 1983), 83.

2. Wright, "The American System of House Building,"

3. Richards Company, *The American System-Built Homes Designed by Frank Lloyd Wright*, promotional brochure, 1916, Frank Lloyd Wright Foundation Archives.

4. Henry-Russell Hitchcock, *In the Nature of Materials, 1887–1941: The Buildings of Frank Lloyd Wright* (Duell, Sloan and Pearce, 1942), 67.

5. Contract between Frank Lloyd Wright and the Richards Company, November 1916, Frank Lloyd Wright Foundation Archives (hereafter cited as Wright-Richards contract).

6. Wright-Richards contract.

7. *Chicago Sunday Tribune*, July 8, 1917, newspaper clipping in Frank Lloyd Wright Foundation Archives, 1506.162.

8. Wright-Richards contract.

9. Wright, *An Autobiography*, 175–224; Kathryn Smith, "Frank Lloyd Wright and the Imperial Hotel: A Postscript," *Art Bulletin* 67, no. 2 (June 1985), 296–310.

10. Anthony Alofsin, *Frank Lloyd Wright: The Lost Years, 1910–1922* (University of Chicago Press, 1993), 70.

11. Du Fresne McArthur, *Frank Lloyd Wright*, 83.

12. Frank Lloyd Wright, "To the Young Man in Architecture—a Challenge," *Architectural Forum*, January 1938.

Chapter 7. The Timeline

1. Mary Jane Hamilton, *Frank Lloyd Wright and Madison: Eight Decades of Artistic and Social Interaction* (Chazen Museum of Art, 1990); Alofsin, *Wright: Lost Years*, 70.

2. A not-for-profit group called Frank Lloyd Wright's Burnham Block is raising money to acquire and renovate most of the buildings.

3. Frank Lloyd Wright to Robert R. Elsner Jr., 19 September 1955, FicheID E084C06, Frank Lloyd Wright Foundation Archives.

4. Juanita M. Ellias, "Prairie School Architecture in Milwaukee: Russell Barr Williamson" (master's thesis, University of Wisconsin–Milwaukee, 1974), 79.

5. Du Fresne McArthur, *Frank Lloyd Wright*, 45.

6. Ellias, "Prairie School Architecture in Milwaukee," 78.

7. Russell Barr Williamson Jr., *Russell Barr Williamson Architect—A Collection* (The Barr Brand, 2000), 132.

Chapter 9. The Delay

1. *Herman F. Krause, Jr., Plaintiff v. Elizabeth Murphy, et al., Defendants*, Case 56124, Summons and Complaint, October 1, 1919, State of Wisconsin, Milwaukee County, Milwaukee County Historical Society.

2. *Herman F. Krause, Jr., Plaintiff v. Elizabeth Murphy, et al., Defendants*, Case 56124, Answer of Defendant, November 11, 1919, State of Wisconsin, Milwaukee County, Milwaukee County Historical Society.

3. "Building Contract," FLWFA Specs Box 2 1112-1903, Frank Lloyd Wright Foundation Archives.

4. *Krause v. Murphy et al.*, Summons and Complaint.

5. *Krause v. Murphy et al.*, Answer of Defendant.

6. Henry Nicholls, "Pandemic Influenza: The Inside Story," *PLOS Biology* 4, no. 2 (February 2006): e50.

7. Dorothy Hoffmann, conversation with the author, January 25, 2020.

Chapter 10. The Finding

1. Blair Kamin, "The Mysterious 29," *Chicago Tribune*, July 6, 2018.

2. Pat Wisialowski, conversations with the author, December 2016.

3. Michael Horne, email to Julilly Kohler, July 2013.

4. Michael Horne, conversations with the author, April 2019.

5. Horne, conversations with the author. William Allin Storrer also used the word *pariah* in reference to Wright's possible work on a series of Prairie School homes built in River Forest, Illinois, in 1913. Storrer describes a cooperative search for these lost homes with Richard Johnson and Dominique Watts called the "Rediscovering Wright Project." William Allin Storrer, *The Architecture of Frank Lloyd Wright: A Complete Catalog*, 4th ed. (University of Chicago Press), 182.

6. Horne, conversations with the author and "Shorewood's 'New' Frank Lloyd Wright Home."

7. Frank Lloyd Wright, *A Testament* (Bramhall House, 1957), 19.

Chapter 11. The Scare

1. We learned subsequently that Wright did not call out pebble dash or roughcast in the American System-Built Home specifications; he called only for stucco. "Specifications of Materials."

2. Byrkit was actually spelled with one *t* but misspelled "Byrkitt" in the specification documents. "Specifications of Materials."

3. Byrkit-Hall Sheathing Lath Co., "How to Build a Warm, Strong and Dry House" (1890), company brochure, https://archive.org/details/HowToBuildAWarmStrongAndDryHouseByrkitsPatentSheathingLath/mode/2up.

4. "Specifications of Materials."

5. Sarah Downey, "Wright House, Wrong Neighborhood," *Chicago Reader*, May 30, 2002.

6. "600 Fillmore," Gary—America's Magical Industrial City, http://www.chameyer.net/600fillmore.html.

7. Nikolas Vakalis, *House B-1 American System-Built Homes—Restoration of the Finishing* (Technical Research and Specification Report, February 2006), Wisconsin Historical Society.

Chapter 12. The Records

1. The total number of models planned remains a mystery. As new documents are uncovered, model numbers can be added to a list of ideas but may lack a supporting drawing or ledger reference in the museum collection. For example, Wright himself listed the models B107, J531, and J801 in correspondence, but the Avery collection does not include a drawing for or a reference to these designs. *Frank Lloyd Wright v. The Richards Company, a Wis corp. and The Richards Company a Delaware Corporation*, Exhibit 2: Correspondence between Frank Lloyd Wright and Emerson Ela, Dane County Circuit Court Case Files, Dane Series 109, Box 386, Wisconsin Historical Society.

2. Storrer, *Architecture of Frank Lloyd Wright*, 215–31.

3. Du Fresne McArthur, *Frank Lloyd Wright*, 5.

4. John O. Holzhueter, "Frank Lloyd Wright's Designs for Robert Lamp," *Wisconsin Magazine of History* 72, no. 2 (1989), 109.

5. The Wright apprentice and noted Minnesotan architect John H. Howe saved and later framed artifacts that he collected while at Taliesin, including American System-Built renderings drawn by Rudolph Schindler and Antonin Raymond. John Howe Papers, MSS 842, Box 47, State Historical Society of Wisconsin Archives Division.

6. Grant Carpenter Manson, *Frank Lloyd Wright to 1910: The First Golden Age* (Reinhold, 1958), 204.

7. The complete text of Frank Lloyd Wright's ledger entry for the three A Models 201, 202, and 203 reads, "24 × 40 Living Room with Dining Nook. Kitchen 2 Bed Rooms Side Main Entry & Service Entry Fireplace Stairs to Basement." An additional note for Model A202 reads, "Same as 201 Except Gable Roof." An

additional note for Model A203 reads, "Same as 201 Except Hip Roof." FLWFA Specs Box 2 1112–1903, Frank Lloyd Wright Foundation Archives.

8. Du Fresne McArthur, *Frank Lloyd Wright*, 34.

9. Nicholas Olsberg, "Flat-Pack Wright," *Architectural Review*, 4 September 2015.

10. Arthur L. Richards to Frank Lloyd Wright, 1 January 1917, FicheID R001 C09, Frank Lloyd Wright Foundation Archives.

11. American System-Built Home stewards Debra and David Nemeth, Mike Wilk and Katie Bailey Wilk, Suzanne Bost and Stuart Wick, and Michael Schreiber and Jason Loper, conversations with the author, January 2020.

Chapter 13. The Unraveling

1. Industrially produced plywood was not commercially available until the late 1920s, but starting in the middle of the nineteenth century and with improvements to the rotary lathe, veneers could be cut in large sheets and glued together in layers by lumberyards and cabinet makers. Lesser-grade materials could be sandwiched between select veneers to create good-looking boards at less cost and with less chance of warping. "Plywood," How Products Are Made, http://www.madehow.com/Volume-4/Plywood.html.

2. "Specifications of Materials."

3. Similar handwriting and details have been found on boards in other American System-Built Homes. Mike Wilk and Katie Bailey Wilk, stewards of the H. Howard Hyde House in Chicago, conversations with the author, January 2020.

4. Debra and David Nemeth, stewards of the Guy C. Smith House in Chicago, conversations with the author, October 2018, and Mike Wilk and Katie Bailey Wilk, conversations with the author.

5. Michael Schreiber and Jason Loper, stewards of the Delbert Meier House in Monona, Iowa, conversations with the author, March 2019.

Chapter 14. The Exception

1. We have since added a replica grill to the outside of the house on the south-facing wall where a light opening should have been. The grill is decorative only—light can't pass through it—but it brings visual balance to the asymmetric layout of the front exterior. The grill can be seen on the right side of the 2019 photograph near the end of chapter 4. We plan to do something similar on the east-facing wall but hope it will pass light.

Chapter 15. The Flip

1. Traci Schnell, architectural historian and volunteer board member, Wright in Wisconsin, conversation with the author, March 2017.

2. *Herman F. Krause, Jr., Plaintiff v. Elizabeth Murphy, et al., Defendants*, Case 56124, Stipulation and Order—Dismissing Action, April 12, 1920, State of Wisconsin, Milwaukee County, Milwaukee County Historical Society.

3. Village records show that there were fewer than five hundred homes in Shorewood in 1917.

4. Linda McQuillen, interview by the author, June 2018. McQuillen was the owner of the house at the time of the interview. In fact, the house did not sell in 1918 and was temporarily turned into a rental, and Groves would not continue with the program. Storrer, *Architecture of Frank Lloyd Wright*, 231.

5. Debra and David Nemeth, conversations with the author, January 2020.

6. "Men Planning to Build Subdivisions" materials, FLWFA Specs Box 2 1112–1903, Frank Lloyd Wright Foundation Archives.

7. Wright, "In the Cause of Architecture" (May 1914).

8. Richards to Wright, 1 January 1917.

9. Arthur L. Richards to Frank Lloyd Wright, 6 February 1917, FicheID R001C06, Frank Lloyd Wright Foundation Archives.

10. Richards to Wright, 6 February 1917.

Chapter 16. The Miss

1. Williamson, *Russell Barr Williamson Architect*, 132–33.

2. Ellias, "Prairie School Architecture in Milwaukee," iii.

3. Juanita Ellias, conversation with the author, August 18, 2020.

4. Ellias, "Prairie School Architecture in Milwaukee," 5.

5. Williamson's son wrote that soon after marrying, Russell and Nola Mae Williamson "took up residence in one of the houses on the farm part of Taliesin," though Nola Mae did not approve of the lifestyle she found there. (Wright was living with a woman to whom he was not married.) Williamson, *Russell Barr Williamson Architect*, 3.

6. David E. Link, "Architecture: A Series of Happy Experiences," *Milwaukee Sentinel*, September 14, 1963.

7. Frank Lloyd Wright, "In the Cause of Architecture," *Architectural Record* 23, no. 3 (March 1908), 164.

8. Manson, *Frank Lloyd Wright to 1910*, 173.

9. Dorothy Hoffman, conversations with the author, February 2019. Local lore suggests that Williamson wore an outfit like Wright's as an act of impersonation, but his family biographer suggests otherwise, citing Meryle Secrest, who wrote that the costume was made popular by Elbert Hubbard. Williamson, *Russell Barr Williamson Architect*, 11.

10. Sales Records in the Residential Appraisal Records, Village of Shorewood, Office of the Assessor.

11. Ellias, conversation with the author.

Chapter 17. The Overlap

1. *Krause v. Murphy et al.*, Answer of Defendant.
2. Du Fresne McArthur, *Frank Lloyd Wright*, 30.
3. Ellias, "Prairie School Architecture in Milwaukee," 134.
4. *Krause v. Murphy, et al.*, Summons and Complaint, October 1, 1919.
5. *Krause v. Murphy, et al.*, Answer, October 1, 1919.
6. "Specifications of Materials."
7. Horne, conversations with the author.
8. Lilek, *2106 East Newton Avenue*.
9. *Wright v. Richards Company*.
10. *Wright v. Richards Company*.
11. *Wright v. Richards Company*, Exhibit 2.
12. *Wright v. Richards Company*, Exhibit 2.

Chapter 18. The Pickup

1. Classified advertisement, Realtor.com, https://www.realtor.com/realestateandhomes-detail/2015-E-Beverly-Rd_Milwaukee_WI_53211_M75000-28430#photoo. When streets and houses in Shorewood were renumbered, 427 Beverly became 2015 East Beverly Road.

2. William Allin Storrer, conversation with the author, October 2018. In a subsequent email exchange, he would confirm that attribution to Williamson "looks correct from my viewpoint."

3. Ellias relied on public records for attribution, and none existed for the Beverly house, so she was left to surmise that Williamson was its architect, based on his dealings with Richards and Richards's claims and advertisements. Ellias, conversation with the author.

4. Russell Barr Williamson to Arthur Peabody, 4 August 1919, in Ellias, "Prairie School Architecture in Milwaukee," 124.

5. B-7 drawings were not initialed by Williamson and Harold Richards in 1916, and the model was not included in the 1917 ledger and catalog of available homes, so a Model B-7 was probably never built, and Wright could not have known whether Williamson or Richards possessed drawings.

6. "Belvedere" is the name given to the oversized flat-topped ventilated chimney box on some American System-Built Home drawings, as seen in Frank Lloyd Wright Foundation Archives, 1506.970.

7. *Wright v. Richards Company*, Findings of Fact and Conclusions of Law.

8. Richards continued to experiment with the word *American* in many of his speculations. He would go on to form businesses called "American Builders Services" and "American Realty Services Company," to which Williamson would contribute designs. Williamson, *Russell Barr Williamson Architect*, 131–34.

9. According to Russell Barr Williamson Jr., his father's known portfolio of work includes at least two other Tudor-style homes, one built in 1921 at 2725 East Beverly Road and another built in 1922 at 2709 East Shorewood Avenue. Williamson, *Russell Barr Williamson Architect*, 132.

10. Traci Schnell, interview with the author, January 3, 2018, republished at the website Wright in Racine by Mark Hertzberg, https://wrightinracine.wordpress.com/2015/06/05/newly-discovered-wright-home-near-milwaukee/.

11. There are other homes in Shorewood, Milwaukee, and Wauwatosa credited to Williamson that resemble American System-Built models, but none that can be shown to be as old as the Bellews' home and the house on Beverly. Du Fresne McArthur, *Frank Lloyd Wright*, 73, 71–80.

12. Williamson to Peabody.

13. The article promotes concrete as a poured medium, but the Eggers Bungalow is built from blocks made in a factory. See Russell Barr Williamson, "The Architecture of the Concrete House," *Concrete Magazine*, January 1921, 16.

Chapter 19. The Silence

1. Anthony Alofsin, ed., *Frank Lloyd Wright: An Index to the Taliesin Correspondence* (Garland, 1988).

2. Link, "Architecture."

3. On Sullivan and Schindler, see Bruce Brooks Pfeiffer, ed., *Frank Lloyd Wright: Letters to Architects* (Press at California State University Fresno, 1984).

4. Arthur L. Richards to Frank Lloyd Wright, 11 May 1949, FicheID R065D02, Frank Lloyd Wright Foundation Archives.

5. Jefferson J. Aikin and Thomas H. Fehring, *Historic Whitefish Bay: A Celebration of Architecture and Character* (History Press, 2017), 125.

6. Arthur L. Richards to Frank Lloyd Wright, 20 April 1945, FicheID M139A03, Frank Lloyd Wright Foundation Archives.

Chapter 20. The Submission

1. Wright, "In the Cause of Architecture" (May 1914).

2. Wright, "In the Cause of Architecture" (May 1914).

3. Alofsin, *Wright: Lost Years*, 70.

4. Hitchcock, *In the Nature of Materials*, 67.

5. Williamson, *Russell Barr Williamson Architect*, 5.

6. So-called atmospheric theaters were movie houses designed in the early 1920s to evoke a period or a place. Williamson's version was styled after a Mediterranean villa.

7. "To Break Ground for Shorewood's First Skyscraper," *Lake Shore Radio* 1, no. 29 (February 8, 1929), 1, courtesy of Shorewood Historical Society.

8. Jerry W. Markham, *A Financial History of the United States: From J. P. Morgan to the Institutional Investor* (M. E. Sharpe, 2002), 151.

9. Timothy Samuelson, "10410 and 10541 South Hoyne Avenue, Criteria for designation as historic landmarks submitted to the Commission on Chicago Landmarks," Chicago.gov, 1994, https://archive.org/details/AmericanSystemBuiltHouses-ChicagoLandmarks/.

10. Wright, *A Testament*, 185.

11. Betty Kassler to Frank Lloyd Wright, 11 May 1955, FicheID K118E09, Frank Lloyd Wright Foundation Archives; Frank Lloyd Wright to Betty Kassler, 18 May 1955, FicheID K0019A04, Frank Lloyd Wright Foundation Archives.

Chapter 21. The Legacy

1. Classified advertisement, *Milwaukee Sentinel*, May 2, 1941. The house was advertised as a Wright design each time it was sold until 1992, when it was sold simply as a "6 room ranch with room to grow," presumably for estate reasons.

2. United Nations Educational, Scientific and Cultural Organization (UNESCO), "Two Cultural Sites Added to UNESCO's World Heritage List," July 7, 2019, https://whc.unesco.org/en/news/2006/. The home, called the Herbert and Katherine Jacobs House by UNESCO, was included as one of

eight Wright buildings in the newly designated site titled "The 20th-Century Architecture of Frank Lloyd Wright."

3. Real estate price inflation in the United States is a phenomenon of the period after World War II, so it is not surprising that relative pricing for like-sized homes would remain relatively stable over three decades.

4. Avery Trufelman, "Usonia 1," *99% Invisible*, episode 246, February 7, 2017, audio, 28:20, https://99percentinvisible.org/episode/usonia-1/.

Index

Page numbers in italics indicate illustrations